Selah!
(Pause and consider)

Lynn B Fowler

This book is © Copyright Lynn Fowler 2025

Individual pieces are © Copyright Lynn Fowler from earlier years

This book, or individual pieces from this book, may not be reproduced, except for brief sections for review, without the written consent of the Copyright holder.

Scripture quotations used in this book are taken from the World English Bible

This book is published by KOGMI Books, the publication arm of King of Glory Ministries International

kingofgloryministriesinternational.com

YouTube: youtube.com/@KOGMI

Facebook: facebook.com/KingOfGloryMinistriesInternational

ISBN 978-1-7635737-1-0

*This book is dedicated to
my Lord and Saviour, Jesus Christ,
and to the Church, the Body of Christ,
in the hope that it will spur Christians on
to a deeper relationship with Christ.*

CONTENTS

Introduction 5

But If Not 6

Are You On The Right Bus? 9

Choices 11

Connected to the Vine 14

Be Still 17

Christian Fortune Telling 20

What is Your Point of Increase? 24

Take Hold of Your Destiny 27

Developing a Kingdom Mindset 31

Developing Passion for God 35

A Very Sad End 38

Come Into the Ark 40

Don't Do The Devil's Job For Him 43

Is Christmas Pagan? 47

Eight Reasons to Praise the Lord 50

What Should the Prophets Speak? 54

CONTENTS (Cont)

Extravagant Love 57

His Word Above His Name 61

Faith and Fire 64

Faithful Servants 69

Two Maligned Bible Women 72

Beyond Imagination 75

Are You a Disciple or Just a Fan? 77

Is it a God Idea or Just a Good Idea? 80

Gratitude: The Power to Change Lives 83

Has the Cloud Moved? 87

Incarnate 90

How Many Cities? 92

How to Wreck a Party 95

I Know the Plans I Have For You 98

In the Name of Jesus 101

War I Heaven 104

It is Finished! 106

CONTENTS (Cont)

Of Lame Ducks and Eagles 109

Pray Impossible Prayers 112

Law and Grace 114

Living in the Anointing 120

More Than a Blind Eye 123

New Beginnings 126

Pregnant With A Promise 129

Prestidigitation 132

Set Apart 139

Substitute 142

The Camel's Nose Principle 145

The Challenge 151

The Gods We Create 154

Together in the Storm 157

The King's Friend 159

What Does Revival Look Like? 162

The Other Side of Death 164

CONTENTS (Cont)

Jesus: What Kind of Man Is This (Part 1) 169

Jesus: What Kind of Man is This (Part 2) 174

Where's The Salt? 178

Who Raided The Ark While It Was Lost? 183

Wise Men Still Seek Him 188

You're Not Home Yet! 191

The Fear of the Lord 194

Meet the Author 197

INTRODUCTION

Thank you for choosing this book. The articles, stories and poems included here have been written over many years, and have been previously published either in print magazines or books, or online. As I have read back over them I have come to the conviction that they still have something to offer to the Body of Christ. I have brought them together in this collection in the hope that they will stir believers to think more deeply about their faith and their relationship with the Lord Jesus Christ.

Most Christians will be familiar with the term Selah, used often in the Psalms, and meaning "pause and consider." That's exactly what I want my readers to do, so I thought it would be the perfect title for this book.

I pray you will be blessed by this book. I have included the links for King of Glory Ministries International's web site and social media pages on the copyright page. If God uses this book to minister into your life, I would love for you to contact me through any of those pages and share your experience.

In Kingdom service,

Lynn B. Fowler

BUT IF NOT...

For many years, the teaching on faith in many churches has gone something like this: "God's Word says that He (heals/ provides/ delivers/ protects ...) You need (healing/ provision/ deliverance/ protection ...) Just believe and you will receive."

There is a large element of truth in this. God does not change. Jesus is the same yesterday, today and forever. In the Gospels, Jesus healed every person who came to Him in faith, and every person who was brought to Him by the faith of others. It is reasonable, then that we would expect Him to heal every person who comes to him in faith today.

Likewise, the Bible shows God providing for His people. It shows Him delivering them in times of adversity, setting them free from spiritual bondages, and protecting them from the attacks of both human and spiritual enemies. Since He is no respecter of persons - He did not favour the people of 2000 and more years ago more than those of today - we could reasonably expect that He would act the same way toward the people of the early 21st century.

Much of the time, that is exactly what He does. When we come to Him in faith and present our requests, He responds positively and meets our needs.

Yet there can be few Christians who have not experienced the opposite at some time in their Christian walk. They need healing. They have prayed. They have had others pray. They have received the laying on of hands, and perhaps anointing with oil. They have searched out and claimed every Scripture relating to healing. They have confessed wholeness. They have bound the spirit of infirmity, they have cut off curses, they have cancelled demonic assignments. They have commanded their bodies to come into line with the Word of God.

Still nothing happens. Their bodies continue to hurt. The cancer continues to spread. The paralysed limbs continue to refuse to move.

Someone says, "Oh, but you have received healing in the spirit realm." Big deal! They want it in the physical realm. They want a body that works.

The issue may not be physical healing. It may be any of the other areas in which we believe for God to move on our behalf, because we know that we are beyond the place where we can help ourselves: financial relief for the person staggering under a load of debt; the restoration of a relationship that is hanging by a thread; protection in the face of injustice and persecution. In any one of those areas we either know or have heard of people who have experience God's miraculous intervention. If we are honest, we will admit that we also know or have heard of people who have not.

The question is not, do we believe God is able to intervene. It is, what will we do if He chooses not to intervene. Will we throw a tantrum and go off to sulk? Will we tell God that He doesn't really love us (in spite of abundant evidence to the contrary)? Will we lose faith, if not in God Himself then at least in His ability to heal/ provide/ deliver/ protect or whatever?

This was the question that once confronted three young men. Snatched from their home and family and dragged off to a foreign country, they had nonetheless risen to a place of prominence in that country's public service. Then came the crunch. The king set up a massive idol, and commanded that at a given signal everyone in the country was to bow before it.

Anyone who did not would be sentenced to an horrendous death. The three young men, however, were worshippers of the true God, and to them the idea of bowing before a heathen idol was absolutely unthinkable.

When their defiance of the king's decree was discovered, they were hauled before him. Without mincing words, he told them that they would either bow before his statue or face the furnace.

They knew that the God they served was able to deliver them out of this impossible situation, and did not hesitate to tell the king so. Yet they were also prepared to bow before the will of God. He was not their servant, they were His. They admitted to themselves the possibility that He would, for reasons only He could understand, choose not to deliver them in this situation. They remembered the prophets who had gone before them, many of whom had given their lives in their witness for God.

So it was that Shadrach, Meshack and Abednego, three young lads from a conquered nation, stood before Nebuchadnezzar, the most powerful king in the world of that day, and declared, "Our God is able to rescue us. We believe He will rescue us. But even if He doesn't, we won't bow before your idol."

But if not... God is able to heal me, I believe He will heal me, but if not, I will still serve Him. God is able to provide for me, I believe He will, but if not I will still not go after other gods. God is able to come up with the miracle I need in whatever situation I happen to be in, but if I never see the miracle, I will still cling to God.

Basically, it comes down to what is most important to us - God Himself, or the things He can do on our behalf.

ARE YOU ON THE RIGHT BUS?

Quite a few years ago, I was travelling by interstate bus from Brisbane to Melbourne. On these buses, travellers are allotted set seat numbers with their tickets. I had arrived early and found my seat just in time to watch this small drama unfold. A man was already settled into the seat immediately in front of mine, when another man boarded and wandered down the aisle looking at seat numbers. Finally he stopped, looked at the man seated in front of me, and said that the seat was his. A fairly strong disagreement broke out, with both men flashing their tickets and insisting that the seat was theirs. Finally, the second man went back into the terminal and returned with a lady from the bus company office to settle the dispute. After looking at the first man's ticket, she regarded him solemnly for a moment before delivering her verdict: "Yes, Sir, you are definitely in the right seat. Unfortunately, you are on the wrong bus!"

Many people in the world today are "in the right seat" but on the "wrong bus." They have faith, but their faith is not based in truth. They "believe in God" but have never found the reality of Who God is, or how He is to be approached. They pray, but their prayers are not directed to the only true Source of power. They look for salvation, but have never come to the Saviour.

A skydiver may have faith in his parachute, that when he pulls the ripcord it will open and successfully slow his decent toward earth so that he can land safely. However, if his parachute has been incorrectly packed, or if someone has tampered with it, it may not function properly. No matter how much faith the skydiver has, it will not prevent him from plunging to his death.

Likewise many a small boy has launched himself off a rooftop or other high spot, believing that if he just flapped his arms hard enough he would be able to fly, only to learn with bruised ego and scraped knees, that little boys were not designed to fly. No matter how passionately he believed it, believing could never make it so.

Jesus said, "I am the way, the truth and the life. No-one comes to the father except through Me." (John 14:6.) If our faith is placed anywhere other than in the Lord Jesus Christ, we are on the wrong bus. It will not take us where we want to go, no matter how much faith we exert. If we believe in a god other than the God Who manifested Himself in the person of the Lord Jesus Christ, we will find ourselves headed in the wrong direction. Our prayers addressed other than through Jesus will not bring us answers, and there is no other who can offer us the reality of salvation.

Some people think that it does not matter what we believe, as long as we are sincere, but being sincere is not enough. There are many people in the world who sincerely wrong. The man sitting in front of me in the bus was sincere, but he was wrong. The prophets of Baal who confronted Elijah on Mount Carmel were sincere, but they were wrong. The misguided young men and women who blow themselves up in suicide bombings are sincere, but they are wrong.

Much as some people don't like the idea, truth is objective. We cannot shape it to our wishes. And it is only when we base our faith on truth, on the reality of Who God is and what He has said, that our faith has any value.

Where is your faith placed? If we place our faith in fantasies and wishes, we will find ourselves going nowhere, but when our faith is firmly placed in God through the Lord Jesus Christ, and based on the truth of God's Word, we begin to move in the right direction.

CHOICES

Every day of our lives we are confronted by choices. For those of us who are blessed to live in developed nations, the number of can be quite daunting. Want a cup of coffee? Will that be cappuccino, latte, short black, long white, cup, mug or demitasse, sugar or sweetener, milk or cream, or any other of a seemingly endless list of possibilities?

Whilst many of the choices demanded of us every day can be every bit as trivial as a cup of coffee, we should not allow their triviality or their sheer volume to distract us from the far more important choices which we also must make each day.

Deuteronomy 30:19 tells us, "Therefore choose life, that you may live, you and your descendants;" Again, Joshua 24:15 says, "choose today whom you will serve."

Those two choices - which are really the same - are the most important we will ever make. God sets before us life and death. Life comes by following and obeying Him, death by rejecting Him and following other gods - including the great god self.

We have become accustomed to thinking of our decision for God as a one-off event. We came to Jesus, repented of our sins, and by faith accepted His death on our behalf and the forgiveness that was bought for us at such an awesome cost, and surrendered our life to Him.

All of that is wonderful, and necessary, but it is only the beginning. An athlete does not win an Olympic gold medal simply by deciding to run. That decision is important - without it he would never even begin toward his goal - but unless he follows it by a series of right choices, the medal will go to someone else. Our athlete must choose to get up and train instead of lazing in bed. He must choose to push his body just that little bit further when everything in him just wants to stop. He must choose to eat healthy food instead of hamburgers and ice cream. He must choose to curtail his social life so that his body gets sufficient rest to allow it to function at maximum capacity. His one large choice - to compete in the Olympics - will not get him over the line, but his daily small choices will.

It is the same with us. As the popular Christian song says, we have decided to follow Jesus. Our goal is not an Olympic medal, but the conformity to the image of Christ which is promised to us in His Word. Our big initial decision will start us toward our goal, but by itself it will not take us over the line. Now we must make all the daily small choices. We must choose to put God first, carving time for prayer and Bible reading out of our busy schedules before anything else. We must choose to become sensitive to the voice of the Holy Spirit, and to respond in obedience to the things He speaks to our heart. We must choose to die to our own ideas of what is right and wrong, and instead embrace the standards set out in the Word of God. We must choose to allow the Spirit of God to shape and mould us, even when the process is anything but comfortable.

By doing all these things we are not earning our salvation. That is God's free grace-gift to us, paid for only by the blood of Jesus shed on our behalf. Rather, we are placing ourselves in the position where God can fulfil His purposes in our lives and transform us into the image of His Son (Romans 8:29). And that, after all, is the real purpose of salvation.

What about your choices? God tells us to choose life - that would seem to most people to be a very obvious choice. Yet the only way we can really choose life is by making those choices that lead to life. Have you made the initial choice to follow Jesus? Are you making the daily choices that give substance to that initial choice?

CONNECTED TO THE VINE

"I am the vine, you are the branches." With those words, Jesus summed up the relationship between Himself and His people, and there are some very important things we can learn from this parable.

The branch shares the life of the vine. As long as it is part of the vine, it has everything it needs. Its nourishment comes through the vine, it doesn't have to go out seeking for water or nutrients for itself, it simply receives them from the vine. Likewise our life comes from Christ, and as long as we are in Him He is able to provide everything we need. We don't have to go off hunting for other sources to have our needs met. How sad that so many people do just that!

At the same time, although the branch's nourishment comes from the vine, the branch has to do something with it. It has to have its leaves out to catch the sun and begin the wonderful process of photosynthesis which turns the raw nutrients into that which is needed for the vine's growth. Likewise our growth in God is a co-operative process. We cannot do it by ourselves without the Lord, but He will not do it by Himself without our co-operation. God is not in the magic wand business! Sometimes our co-operation will be simply a matter of reaching out and taking hold, by faith, of what He has provided for us. At other times we will need to be more pro-active, earnestly seeking God through prayer and the Word, and then doing what He tells us to do.

The branch shares the identity of the vine. People do not look at a branch and say, "That's a branch of a grapevine". Rather, they look and say, "That's a grape vine." In fact, the only time when the branches have an identity of their own is when they have been cut off from the vine and no longer share in its life. Some Christians have great difficulty with the concept that when the world looks at us, it should be able to see Jesus. Yet if we share then identity of the vine that should be natural and inevitable.

In sharing the identity of the vine, the branches share the character of the vine. It is natural for the branches of a grape vine to bear grapes. It is not natural for the branches of a grape vine to bear lemons. The branch does not have to struggle and strive and turn itself inside out saying, "I must bear grapes not lemons, I must bear grapes not lemons..." It simply bears grapes. Yet so many of us struggle to bear the fruit of the Spirit. Why?

The branch also shares the life of the other branches. The healthiness of each is a measure of the health of the vine as a whole. Likewise we share the life of the whole Body of Christ. Throughout the New Testament, God makes it clear that we cannot live our lives in isolation. What one member of the Body does affects the other members. Therefore we are to pray for one another, to bear one another's burdens, to weep when another weeps and to rejoice when he rejoices.

Sometimes dead branches remain on the vine, still attached but no longer drawing life from the vine. Likewise there are many who are visibly part of the church, but are dead branches. They do not draw their life from Christ. Some never did, going to church only from ritual or tradition or a works mentality. Others have let their relationship with God wither, till they no longer share in His life but remain only to be seen as part of the vine.

The branches need the vine, the vine does not need the branches. God is a good gardener, and sooner or later He will prune off those who no longer share the life of the vine. This does not destroy the vine, but rather makes it flourish. At one of the houses where we lived when my kids were teenagers, we had an ancient grape vine growing over a pergola. One year I decided to prune it, and with far more zeal than knowledge I was totally ruthless. My kids looked at it sadly and said, "Mum, that thing will never grow grapes again!" How wrong they were! We had more grapes off that vine that year than we had ever had before. In the same way, when God prunes the church it brings growth. Remember Ananias and Sapphira? They had lost their connection with the vine, and God pruned them. The result was growth for the church. In our personal lives also, there are times when God will prune us. This is not to destroy us, but to cause us to bring forth more fruit.

Sharing the life of the vine, sharing the identity and character of the vine, should be for branches the most natural thing in the world. So why do so many of us find it so difficult? Why is it that for so many of us, messages like this are just a nice theory that doesn't work out in the reality of life?

I believe the answer lies in the fact that we are not natural branches, but grafted branches. Many of us are only half grafted! Part of us is still attached to the old root stock, and we are drawing our life from two different sources. We need to cut off the old root stock, let it die, and allow the Lord to fully graft us into Christ.

BE STILL

It was a soft summer night, pleasantly cool with just enough breeze to cause the little glass bells that hang in my window to tinkle gently. The air was heavy with the vibrant, living silence that is known only in the country. I was busy unpicking a garment I had knitted and then decided I didn't like, an occupation which required my hands but little of my attention. A sweet, gentle presence of God settled over the whole room, and I found myself filled with a deep sense of peace and contentment as I nestled into Him. I was still. I was not really praying as such, simply enjoying His presence. I dare to believe that He was enjoying my company, too. It was a precious time of heart communion, to the extent that I was very reluctant to get up and go to bed.

Be still. It is one of those directives from God that we sometimes find it so difficult to obey. We are so caught up in our busy-ness, so task-oriented, that simply being still is quite foreign to us. We rush through moments, days and years, barely sensible of their passing. There is so much happening! How often have we reached the end of a year, only to look back and think, "It was such a *busy, full* year! But where did it go?"

Even our prayer is busy. There are so many things we need to bring before the Throne of Grace – both our own needs and those of others. And then, prayer has to be fitted into our busy schedule. It must be efficient, making the most of the time available.

Often we struggle with our Christian walk. We know that we continually fall abysmally short of God's standard, which is His glory, and we wrestle to bring ourselves "up to scratch".

We have a goal in God, and we strive toward it.

God is calling us to be still. Take time to savor this moment: the warmth of the sun or the cool of the rain; the sounds or the silence; the stillness or the movement around us; the physical sensation of whatever we may be doing, whether it is sitting in an armchair or digging in the garden. We will never have this moment again, and even as we touch it, it is gone. Why waste it by filling it with the regrets of the past, or the anxieties of the future?

More importantly, God is calling us to "be still" in our relationship with Him. Our part in the grace equation is to yield to the working of the Holy Spirit within us, not to try to do it ourselves. In fact, the minute we try to do it ourselves we have let go of grace and moved back into works!

Of course, we can't always stop what we are doing to enjoy that moment of stillness. In fact, true stillness doesn't require us to stop. We can enjoy true stillness in the midst of our busy-ness, even in the midst of battle, struggle, oppression and persecution. At one time Jesus said to His disciples, "Come away by yourselves and rest a while." The climbed into a boat and set off to what they thought was going to be a quiet place where they could relax together, but when they got there there was wall-to-wall people! Instead of resting, Jesus launched into a prolonged teaching session. By the time He had finished, it was too late for the people to buy food, so he miraculously fed them with loaves and fishes which He multiplied. (Mark 6:31-44). What went wrong? Did Jesus not know that the crowd would run ahead of them and be waiting for them at their "quiet place"? Did He miss it? Not at all! He was trying to teach them, and us, that true stillness does not depend on the external props, nice though they are. True stillness comes from within. Our real "quiet place" is in our heart.

Likewise Psalm 46 speaks of war and turmoil and God's judgments on the earth, but in the midst of it all He says, "Be still, and know that I am God." (Ps 46:10) True stillness is a centering on God which knows that, no matter what is going on around us, God is in control. A thousand years from today we will not even remember the things which are such a trouble to us at this moment. True stillness is living in the present in the light of the eternal.

Like everything in our Christian walk, it will not happen automatically. Nor will it happen instantly. Stillness needs practice. We need to make choices. Like the Psalmist, we need to command our soul, "My soul, wait in silence for God alone" (Ps. 62:5) Like Jesus in the wilderness, we need to respond to the demons of anxiety with Scripture: "It is written, 'In nothing be anxious, but in everything, by prayer and petition with thanksgiving, let your requests be made known to God. '" (Phil 4:6) We can begin by taking brief moments to stop in the midst of what we are doing and focus on God, drawing into His presence. In time we will not need to stop, merely to refocus. Eventually, we will not even need to do that, for focus on the Lord will have become the normal state of our heart, and we will find ourselves living and working out of a center of stillness deep within us.

CHRISTIAN FORTUNE TELLING

This has been on my heart for some time, and it has reached the point where I can no longer hold back from saying it: much of what passes for "prophecy" in the Church today is really nothing more than "Christian fortune telling."

Before I go any further, let me say very emphatically that I am not anti-prophecy. I move in the gift of prophecy, and some have recognised me as a prophet. Whether I am or not is really irrelevant here, the point I am seeking to make is simply that I believe in both the gift of prophecy and the office of prophet as being relevant and important for today. What bothers me greatly is the way that gift and office is used, or rather misused.

The first thing we need to understand is the difference between prophecy in the Old Testament and prophecy under the New Covenant. In the OT, the people did not have the Holy Spirit as an abiding presence in their lives. He simply came upon individuals to empower them for whatever task God had called them to do. The ordinary people also did not have ready access to the written law. In fact, by the time of Josiah it seems even the priests did not have the Book of the Law, as there was great consternation when it was found during Josiah's repairs to the temple (2Kings 22:8ff.) Because of this, if the people wanted to know what God was saying to them, the only way they could do so was by going to the prophet. The prophet therefore carried the responsibility of hearing from God both on behalf on individuals and on behalf of the nation. When a prophet came to town there was often great excitement, with people eager to receive a word from God.

Under the New Covenant, everything changes. When a person

is born again, the Holy Spirit comes to live in his/her spirit. He is closer to us than our breath. We are meant to be hearing from Him God's direction for our lives. What's more, particularly in our modern age and especially in western nations, we have ready access to the written Word of God, which should be our first touchstone and measure of truth, and of understanding God's character and ways. The function of the prophet in the New Covenant is not to hear from God on your behalf! Personal prophecy should come only as a confirmation of what God has already spoken in our own hearts, a preparation for what He is about to speak, or a rebuke if He has been speaking and we have not been listening.

Instead, we see Christians acting like Old Testament believers. The prophet comes to town and everyone gets excited because they want to get a word from God. (Interesting that, on the whole, Christians don't get nearly as excited when a teacher comes to town.) The prophet promises that everyone in the room will receive a word - something that never happened, even in the Old Testament. The statement is "God always wants to speak to us." That is absolutely true, God does always want to speak to us, but He wants to do so through His Word and His Spirit who lives within us speaking directly to us personally, not through someone else hearing on our behalf. I often think that the only thing God really wants to say to most of the people in the room at these meetings is, "Stop seeking a second-hand experience and start listening to My Spirit for yourself!"

A great problem comes because of the way prophecy is taught. I have been in "Schools of the Spirit" where people are told to look in their hearts to find a word of the people over whom they are prophesying (and I have had some incredibly "off" prophecies over me as a result of this method.) THE TROUBLE IS, THIS IS THE SAME METHOD I WAS TAUGHT WHEN I WAS A SPIRITUALIST MEDIUM

LEARNING TO DO "READINGS." True prophecy does not come by searching inside ourselves. 2Pe 1:21 *"For no prophecy ever came by the will of man: but holy men of God spoke, being moved by the Holy Spirit."* True prophecy comes when the Holy Spirit speaks to the prophet to bring a word to someone, not when the prophet goes digging around in search of a word.

This kind of digging can also lead to "cold reading" a technique practised by stage magicians in which they will make a statement and watch the subject closely for tiny, subtle responses, which then lead to further statements by the magician. Someone skilled in this technique can come up with some amazingly accurate "readings" but they do not come from God, but only from the magician's ability. Unfortunately I have seen this technique used, knowingly or unknowingly, by some who claim the office of prophet.

Church, wake up! Prophecy is a wonderful gift of the Holy Spirit, but it was never meant to be used as Christian fortune telling.

Now I see something in the Church that disturbs me even more: some Christians are using cards to do "readings" for people. I understand these are not traditional tarot cards, but the principle is the same. It is divination: using a physical means to try to "channel" revelation. Whether it is examining the entrails of an animal, reading tea leaves, palm reading, tarot, or these Christian cards it is the same essential practice, and God absolutely forbids and condemns it, going to the extent of calling it (and those who practice it) an abomination. (Deut 18:9-12.) Think that's only for the Old Testament? Revelation 22:15 places "sorcerers" (those who practice divination) among those who are excluded from heaven.

These deluded Christians think that by using these means they are bringing people into the kingdom of heaven, when in reality they are opening them up to the kingdom of darkness. You cannot do God's work using the devil's tools!

Psychic readings are the devil's counterfeit of the Holy Spirit's gifts of word of wisdom, word of knowledge, and prophecy. Christians should not be trying to counterfeit the devil's counterfeit.

Again I say, Church, wake up! Learn to use God's gifts, God's way. Doing things the devil's way can only lead to disaster, both for you personally and for those to whom you seek to minister.

WHAT IS YOUR POINT OF INCREASE?

I love to crochet, but I sometimes find written patterns hard to follow, so I often watch video tutorials. Recently I was watching a tutorial for a shawl when the instructor said, "This is your point of increase." I hadn't heard that specific term before, but I knew what she meant. The point of increase is the point on each row of the pattern where you do something different to ensure that each row will be longer than the previous one, building up to the triangular shape of the shawl.

Some time later, during my prayer time, I felt the Holy Spirit ask, "What is your point of increase?" Obviously He was talking about my spiritual life, not my crochet. I found myself wondering, *Do I have a point of increase? Is there something that I do every day to ensure that every day in the future my spiritual life will be deeper, higher, broader than it is today?*

God never intended our Christian life to be static. Jesus talked about faith like a grain of mustard seed. Most of the time we miss the point of that teaching. Yes, He was saying that even the tiniest amount of faith can bring about amazing things. But to make that point He could just as easily have talked about faith the size of a grain of sand. Instead, He chose a seed: a seed is living, and it has the potential for growth. In fact, it is more than just potential – the only way a seed can not grow is if it is dead. Growth is the very essence of what the seed is about.

It's the same with our spiritual life. It is meant to grow. Paul rebuked the Corinthian church because they were still behaving like babies, not wanting to grow in their faith and go on to maturity. (1 Cor 3:1-2) I'm sure we all know people who were saved 30, 40, or 50 years ago, but are spiritually still babies. Rather than having been Christians for 30, 40, or 50 years, they have been Christians for one year 30, 40, or 50 times over.

So the question comes back for each of us: *What is our point of increase?*

I know that over the past year or two the Lord has been drawing me into an increasingly narrow path. He has greatly increased my time in the Word each day – but that has limitations, because there is only a limited time available. So, whilst extra time in the Word is great, it is not something that can go on increasing. My point of increase has to be something that is not limited by the finite-ness of human existence. Something that is not so much about *doing* as about *being*.

There are things that I could do a year ago – not bad things, just spiritually irrelevant things – that He will no longer allow me to do. I'm sure that refining will continue as He draws me close and closer to Himself. Is that my point of increase? Probably partially – but not totally.

The more I think and pray about it, the more I feel that the real point of increase is the same for all of us: our passion, our zeal, our hunger for the Lord. Moses, who had performed amazing miracles before Pharaoh, who had seen the parting of the Red Sea, who had been up the mountain as it quaked with the presence of the Lord, still cried out to God, "Please show me Your glory." (Ex 33:18)

Paul, to whom God had given the great revelation of His grace, who had seen incredible miracles and had taken the Gospel to a large part of the known world, still declared, "That I may know Him!" (Phil 3:10) The point of increase for both Moses and Paul was that, no matter how much of God and His power they had experienced, they wanted more.

May God give all of us that ever-increasing hunger that will never be satisfied, no matter how great a relationship with God we have today, but will always be pressing in to go deeper, to reach higher, to know more of Him.

TAKE HOLD OF YOUR DESTINY

In Philippians 3:12b, Paul writes, "I press on, that I may take hold of that for which also I was taken hold of by Christ Jesus." Paul was a man of destiny. He knew that God had called him for a purpose, and he was single-minded in pressing toward that goal.

There were many things which could have distracted him, many "good" ideas which he could have followed after, but his mind was set: "One thing I do," he wrote. Not the dozens of things which clamored for his attention each day, not the tantalizing side tracks he could have so easily wandered down, just "one thing." Of course, that does not mean that Paul neglected his commitments in the day-to-day world. We know that for at least part of his ministry he supported himself as a tent-maker. That work obviously required his attention. However, it was not his focus. It was not his "career". It was just a job through which God provided the means for him to continue in the ministry of the Gospel.

Likewise, there was much in the past which could have held Paul back or caused him to detour from his path. In the natural, his past had held success, recognition, acceptance, comfort – it would have been easy for Paul, like the people of Israel when they left Egypt, to look back over his shoulder and yearn for that which had once been. On the other hand, spiritually his past held the guilt of having persecuted the church, even hauling the servants of God off to gruesome deaths, and standing in approval at the death of Stephen. Had Paul allowed the devil to throw up his past, he could well have decided that he was totally unworthy and unfit to be a messenger of the Gospel. However, Paul knew better than to allow either the success or the failure of the past to hold him back from his course. "Forgetting what is behind," he wrote. To Paul, the past was past. What he was doing in the present was what was important.

Paul could also have been distracted in another way. Since God had confronted him on the Damascus Road, a great deal had happened in his life. He had preached in many places and seen them open up to the Gospel. He had reaped a harvest of many souls for the Kingdom. There were churches throughout the known world that related to him, and accepted his apostolic authority. He had been used to bring the "new" revelation of salvation by grace alone to the church, and his teachings were accepted and honoured throughout the Christian world. It would have been easy for Paul to settle down, to consider that he had "arrived", and to begin to take things easy. Yet Paul knew that he had not "made it". "Brothers," he wrote, "I don't regard myself as yet having taken hold, but one thing I do: Forgetting the things which are behind, and stretching forward to the things which are before, 14 I press on toward the goal for the prize of the high calling of God in Christ Jesus." Paul had his eyes fixed on eternity. No matter how far he would progress in his personal relationship with God, no matter how greatly he was used in ministry, there would always remain a "pressing on".

What was "it" that Paul did not consider himself to have yet taken hold of, but which he so ardently pursued? It was his destiny, "that for which Christ Jesus took hold of me."

What is your destiny in God? There are at least three ways we need to consider this. Firstly, every one of us is individually destined to be like Jesus. Romans 8:29 tells us, "Those God foreknew He also predestined to be conformed to the likeness of His Son." What an awesome destiny! God has determined to take each one of us, with all our sin, all our failures, all our defeats, all our hurts, all our baggage, and transform us to be like Jesus. We don't have to do it. We don't have to struggle to "be good". All we have to do is say "Yes" to God, and then allow His Holy Spirit to have His way in our lives as He begins the work of transformation. Yes, sometimes it will be painful, but if we yield to the Spirit of God He will carry us through it. It was written of Jesus that "For the joy that was set before Him endured the Cross" (Heb 12:2). Surely the joy of knowing that one day we will be truly like Him is worth whatever we may have to endure along the way? Surely this is a destiny which we should find so desirable that we put aside the past and press single-mindedly toward this goal?

The second aspect of our destiny is corporate. God did not just save individuals through Jesus' death at the Cross. He defeated the kingdom of satan and brought to birth a new entity, the church, which He describes as the Body of Christ. Have you ever seen those pictures where someone takes the head of one person and places it on the body of another? They never look right, do they? That's because the body is meant to be like the head. When people see your body, they normally recognise you, even if they can't see your head. That's what it is supposed to be like for the church. As Christ's body, we are supposed to look like our head, Jesus. When people look at us, they should recognise Him. Sadly, at the moment that is not always the case. In fact, far too often people are given a very false idea of what God is like by looking at the church. Our corporate destiny, however, is for that likeness to be seen. Ephesians 4:13 tells us that God has placed equipping ministries in the church so that the church may "come to the measure of the stature of the fullness of Christ." God's purpose is that the day will come when, even though people cannot see the head, Jesus, they will see Him in His body. (There are some people who believe that this will not happen till after Jesus returns. However, when Jesus returns His people will be instantly transformed. He will not need equipping ministries to bring us to that place then. Ephesians 4 is talking about what is going to happen before his return!)

Finally, each of us has an individual, personal destiny. God planned you. You were not an accident to him, no matter what the natural circumstances of your birth may have been. Nor did you catch Him by surprise with your birth, leaving Him wondering what on earth He could possibly do with you. No, before ever He created the world He knew that He would create you. He knew exactly what your genetic makeup would be, and what your responses would be to every situation throughout your life. And He planned something special for you – a special role that no-one else can ever do the same way as you can. Yes, if you refuse God's call He will find someone else to do the job – in fact, He already knew you would refuse and already knew who would obey. But that other person will not fulfill that call in the same way you would have. On the other hand, if you accept God's call and obey Him, no matter how much earthly success or failure you may meet, you will always have the satisfaction of knowing that you are doing the very thing for which you were created.

You have a three-fold destiny: to be individually conformed to the likeness of Jesus, to be part of the Body of Christ which is brought into the fullness of the stature of Christ, and to fulfill that unique and special task for which God created and called you. It is a destiny worth pursuing. Will you be like Paul, and allow yourself no distractions from either the past or the present, but set your face toward eternity and with singleness of heart and soul press forward to take hold of that for which Christ Jesus took hold of you?

DEVELOPING A KINGDOM MINDSET

The book of Haggai talks about the time when the people of Israel had returned from their exile in Babylon. They had been back in their own land for a while, and because of opposition and pressure, they had given up on rebuilding the Temple of the Lord, and instead had busied themselves in building their own houses and re-establishing their lives. Things were not going terribly well for them, though. It seemed that everything they put their hands to failed; there was never enough to eat or drink, and their crops never produced the amount they expected. When they worked for someone else, they found their wages disappeared far faster than they could earn them.

God sent the prophet Haggai into this situation to rebuke them for being too busy building their own houses, whilst neglecting His. "Is it a time for you yourselves to dwell in your panelled houses, while this house lies waste?" (Haggai 1:4) God made it very clear that this was the reason for all their problems, and if they wanted things to improve, then they had better start paying first attention to His house.

It seems to me that the Church today is not very different from ancient Israel. Far too many Christians are far too busy building their own houses - their own little worlds of comfort and ease - while neglecting the House of God. For too many, church has become something to do "if there is nothing more important or more interesting to do." If you take that attitude, you can be absolutely certain that the devil will always make sure that there is something that seems more important or more interesting than spending time with the Lord. Too many feel that giving to the Lord's work is something they can do "if there is anything left over at the end of the week." Again, that attitude will guarantee that the devil ensures that there is nothing left over, whether it is by waving temptation to buy something you don't need in front of your face, or causing costly accidents and problems that eat up your funds.

These attitudes are greatly disturbing, but there is something that is even more so, and that is the leaders who are too busy building their own kingdoms, and neglect the Kingdom of God.

When John the Baptist announced the coming of Jesus' ministry, he proclaimed, "Repent, for the Kingdom of God is at hand." Jesus began His own ministry with the same words. In fact, He spent more time talking about the Kingdom of God than He did about anything else. And when He gave His disciples a model prayer, the first petition of that prayer was "Your Kingdom come." Why? Because something cataclysmic was in the process of happening: something that would change the world forever.

To understand it, we need to go back to the beginning of creation. God made man and woman in His own image, and gave them a three-fold mandate: to fill, subdue and rule the world. That rulership, however, was never meant to be apart from Him. He was not setting them up as gods over their own kingdom, but as vice-regents over His. It was the devil that came along and suggested to them that they could be gods in their own right, not needing to come under God's authority but ruling their lives just as they pleased. It was, of course, a lie. In rejecting God's good and loving authority over them, they did not get to rule themselves, but rather made both themselves and the world over which God had placed them subject to the harsh and cruel rulership of Satan. The whole universe is, and always will be, God's Kingdom, but earth became a rebel state within that Kingdom, and the kingdom of darkness ruled.

When Jesus came, all that was to be turned on its head. As the

Last Adam, He would undo the rebellion of the first Adam. Where the first Adam tried to become his own god, Christ laid aside His Godhead to come as man. Where the first Adam rebelled, Christ bowed before the Father's will, declaring "Not My will, but Yours." Where the first Adam had handed the rulership of the world over to the devil, Jesus would reclaim that rulership and re-establish the world as a rightful part of the Kingdom of God.

Yes, Jesus died to buy the salvation of mankind, and to pay the price of sin for every individual who has ever lived. Yes, His death secured for us not only eternal life, but healing, deliverance, provision and all the blessings that come with being re-connected to God. But all that is only a small part of the story. Jesus' death was nothing less than a full-scale uprising, the overthrow of the entrenched rebel government, and the creation of a new world order. Never again would Satan have the right to rule on this planet.

Tragically, Satan does still rule in many areas. He is able to do so for only one reason: the Church has defaulted. We have failed to enforce the victory of Jesus. We have allowed a defeated enemy to continue to reign over individuals and nations. And mostly it has happened because many of the leaders in the Body of Christ have been too busy building their own kingdoms to be bothered building the Kingdom of God.

Jesus has won the victory, but He has left it up to us to enforce it. With His return growing closer every day, we cannot afford to keep our narrow focus. We must begin to look at the big picture. We must begin to think and act in ways that will not only build our own ministries, but will build the Kingdom of God.

Look beyond your own house! Ask what God is doing through the brother or sister working down the street. Begin to pray for that one. Pray for them everything you would want for your own ministry. Release blessing and anointing upon them. Rejoice when you hear that they have had a breakthrough, even if you are still waiting for yours. Weep in intercession for their struggles, even if you are riding high on the crest of victory.

Visit that other work and ask what you can do to help build their vision. Seek ways that you can work together to establish the Kingdom of God in your town or city, and beyond that in your nation. Stretch beyond your denominational boundaries.

I was saved in the middle of the Charismatic Movement of the 1970s. I remember a preacher at the time saying that it was as if there had been all these sheep separated into different, fenced-off paddocks. Then the rain of the Spirit had begun, and the flood waters began to rise till they covered the fences, and the sheep were just swimming everywhere. Sadly, the waters receded, and the fences were rebuilt higher and stronger than ever.

It would be nice if God sent another flood of the Spirit to just wash the fences away. But I suspect that this time, we have to first tear the fences down and use the wood to build the House of the Lord.

DEVELOPING PASSION FOR GOD

One of the best-loved passages of the Old Testament is the Shemma: "Hear, Israel: Yahweh is our God. Yahweh is one. You shall love Yahweh your God with all your heart, with all your soul, and with all your might." (Deut 6:4-5). It was this commandment, rather than one of the Ten, that Jesus chose when challenged as to which was the greatest commandment of the law. All the commands of God ask for our obedience, but this one goes far beyond that: this one asks for our passion.

There are many who serve God only out of duty. That is certainly better than not serving Him at all, but it goes nowhere near the kind of relationship that God desires us to have with Him. He desires that every part of our being – spirit, soul and body – should be passionately committed to Him.

How do we develop that kind of relationship with God? How do we fall madly in love with Him? The same way as we would fall in love with another person – by spending time with Him, and getting to know all the wonderful things about Him. Falling in love with a person requires, to some extent, putting on "rose-coloured glasses" - we overlook the faults and problems of that person, seeing only the good points. With God, no rose-coloured glasses are necessary, for He has no faults or problems. All we need to do is to look closer and closer at Him, seeing more and more of His greatness and goodness.

We can begin by looking around us. Romans tells us that, even if we had never had the revelation of God in Scripture, He has placed enough evidence of Himself in the world around us to point us to a rudimentary faith.

Stand outside on a cloudless night and look at the stars. Try to count them. Consider that many of them are many times the size of our sun, and that, although they seem so close to our eyes, they are millions of miles apart. Let them draw you to think abut the greatness of the Creator.

Hold a rose in your hand. Marvel at its delicate perfection. Dwell for a moment on the fact that, whilst it has aspects that make it clearly a rose, and identify it as a particular type of rose, yet it is totally unique. There is no other rose exactly like this one! Consider also that the rose is only one of thousands of kinds of flowers, some big and flashy, others so tiny and delicate that they are barely noticed by man. Allow yourself to worship God both for His creativity and for the diversity of His creation.

We can move then to the Word of God, for though general revelation can point us toward God, only the specific revelation of His Word shows Him clearly. Read again the familiar stories: Noah and the arc, Moses and the deliverance of Israel, the Judges and God's deliverance of the nation, the prophets and God's righteousness. Read not only as stories that you probably know so well, but read to see the character and attributes of God. Let them speak to you afresh of God's power, His glory, His holiness, His justice.

Move on to the New Testament and God's completed revelation in the person of the Lord Jesus Christ. Allow the words of Philippians 2 to move you as you consider that He gave up all the privilege and power of Godhead and clothed Himself with the frailness of humanity in order to come to earth, for the specific purpose of dying in the place of sinful man. Ask the Holy Spirit to make real to you what every step in that process cost. Remind yourself that, even if you had been the only person on the earth who needed salvation, Jesus would have done the same things, just to save you.

Finally, contemplate all that God has done in your own life. Think about the things He did for you before you ever knew Him: His provision, care and protection. Think of the gift of life itself, and of all that He has given you in the course of that life. Most of all, consider how He drew you to Himself, how He arranged the circumstances of your life so that you would ultimately be drawn to surrender to Him and receive all that He was longing to give you.

Ask the Holy Spirit to help you, and spend time in these exercises regularly. As you do, you will find your heart being drawn more and more toward the Lord. You will find yourself falling more and more in love with Him.

A VERY SAD END

Most people know the story of Gideon. If you don't, it is found in the Old Testament, in the Book of Judges chapters 6-8. The Book of Judges covers a very volatile period in the history of Israel. When Joshua, who had led the people into the Promised Land, died, he did not leave a successor. So the people floundered without leadership. They would fall away from God, and into the worship of all the false gods and idols of the people around them, as well as all kinds of immorality and injustice.

God would then respect their wishes and "hand them over" to these false gods, with the result that the neighbouring peoples would attack and oppress them. When Israel tired of this situation, they would cry out to God, and He would raise up a deliverer who would call the people back to God and defeat their enemies. While the deliverer was alive, things would be fine. When he (or, in one case, she) died, the people would revert to their old ways.

Gideon was one such deliverer. He was called by God at a time when Israel was being heavily oppressed by the Midianites. At the time when God called him, he saw himself as nothing: the least member of the least tribe in Israel, hiding in a winepress to thresh his grain so that the Midianites would not come and take it.

God took him and raised him up to be one of the mightiest warriors in Israel's history. He tore down the altars to the false god Baal and conquered the Midianites, bringing Israel into a forty year period of freedom.

Yet after all that, Gideon ended up leading the people back

into the very idolatry from which he had brought them. The story is in Judges 8:23-27. Having acknowledged that God should be the ruler over the nation, rather than himself, Gideon took up a collection of gold earrings, which he melted down and made into an ephod.

An ephod was part of the priestly garments, and was meant to be used in the service of the Lord. Gideon, however, set this one up as an idol, and all Israel came to worship it.

To us it seems fairly obvious that this was just plain stupid. Yet I wonder how often we do the same thing. How often do we, having served the Lord and seen Him move in our lives and the lives of others, end up turning that very service into an idol which we worship instead of the Lord?

COME IN TO THE ARK

Last night I attended a service at a church where I visit from time to time, in addition to my normal fellowship. It was a time of intense worship, and the tangible presence of the Lord was awesome. At one point the pastor leading the meeting said something about pressing in to the Holy of Holies. The minute he said this, the Holy Spirit spoke to my heart and said, "There is another step. What is in the Holy of Holies?" I replied, "The Ark of the Covenant." "Yes," said the Spirit. "Come in to the Ark." At the time I had no idea what that meant, and it was certainly not something I would have thought of myself.

I spent my entire prayer time this morning listening to the Holy Spirit unpack it for me, and I am presenting this unpolished, just as He gave it to me. I believe it is mostly for the Body of Christ, but there are also some personal elements. I believe there are others to whom God wants to extend this invitation, and who will hear it through this message.

* What does it mean, to "come in to the Ark?" This was something that was never done in the natural – in fact it would have been impossible, as the Ark was only around 1.25 metres long and around .75 metre wide - so there was no precedent to work from. What the Spirit was showing me is that the Holy of Holies is the place of God's radiated presence, but the Ark is the place of His residing presence. If the Ark moved out of the Holy of Holies, His presence would move; but His presence remained always in/on the Ark.

* The high priest came into the Holy of Holies once a year, and when he had completed his duties there he left. When you come into the Ark you will not leave, but will remain there forever.

* The Ark contained the tablets of the Law. Was God saying to go back under the Law? I knew that couldn't be the case, as the Word tells us that in Christ we have died to the Law (Rom 7:6) As I sought the Spirit about this He asked me, "What does the Law reveal?" "God's character," I answered. "Yes," He said, "come in to the fullness of God's character." This means intense breaking and refining.

* The Ark also carries God's power. To enter the Ark is to become a carrier of His power. We must be people He can trust with His power – more breaking and refining.

* The presence of the Ark brings both blessing and judgement. The Spirit warned me solemnly, "Unless you are prepared to carry both, don't even think of entering the Ark. You cannot be "nice". You will be both loved and hated."

* The presence of the Ark confronts false gods (1 Sam 5:2-5) Entering the Ark means a whole new level of spiritual warfare – still more breaking and refining.

* It is "by invitation only." The Spirit took me to the story of Esther – even though she was queen, she could only enter the presence of the king if he extended the golden sceptre to her. We can choose to move from the outer court into the Holy Place. We can choose to press in from the Holy Place to the Holy of Holies – God has torn the curtain and made the way open for us. But we can only enter the Ark when He extends the invitation to us.

* The invitation is only extended to those who have already pressed in to the Holy of Holies. It is not possible to move from the Holy Place in to the Ark, or even to receive the invitation whilst still in the Holy Place. The Holy Place is a place of service, but we have to move from the place of

service as a function to the place of service in and from His presence before we can go deeper.

* That doesn't mean that we can earn or deserve the invitation by being in the Holy of Holies. It just means that by being there we position ourselves to a place where we can either receive or not receive the invitation, just as Esther had to stand at the door to see if the king would extend the golden sceptre to her, but her standing there didn't mean it would automatically happen.

* To touch the Ark means death (2 Sam 6:7), to enter it means ultimate death. In my life and ministry there have been many times of dying to self, but somehow it seems this is the ultimate level of that, and accepting the invitation means a deeper level of surrender than anything I have ever experienced.

Lord, I am humbled and awed by Your invitation. I can't do this, but You can. I accept. I come.

DON'T DO THE DEVIL'S JOB FOR HIM

Last week I listened to a Christian teaching which disturbed me greatly. What bothered me was not the subject, nor the speaker's presentation, but the fact that within the course of a 50-minute sermon this man named and tore down four other ministers or ministries. In two of the cases, he even seemed to take considerable delight in the fact that they had been sued for large sums of money because people had been injured in their meetings.

The Word of God tells us that the devil is "the accuser of the brethren." It is a job that he does very well. Why is it that some Christians feel that they must assist the devil in his work? Our job is not to accuse the brethren, but to uphold, love and encourage them.

To publicly tear down another minister or ministry is to rise up in pride and self-righteousness. It is effectively saying, "I have all the truth, and if you don't agree with me you couldn't possibly be right." The problem is, none of us has all the truth, and many of the "truths" that we hold dear are in fact not the truth, but merely our interpretation of it. For instance, two hundred years ago many Christians in the western world believed it to be a truth that the Bible not only permitted but encouraged slavery. There are very few today who would not see that that "truth" was in fact filtered through the lenses of self-interest, and was a serious distortion of what the Word actually says. On the other hand, sometimes two apparently opposite truths are in fact both aspects of the one whole. For instance, Paul taught salvation by grace through faith, not of works, whilst James taught that faith without works is dead. They were not teaching conflicting doctrines, but rather the two sides of the same truth. Our first response when someone is teaching something with which we disagree should be to ask the Lord to show us if they are right and we are wrong, or if perhaps we each are seeing a different side of the same coin.

To publicly tear down another minister or ministry violates the law of love. Jesus' command to us was that we love one another. Love is not just a word or a feeling, but encompasses the areas of practical concern and support. If we feel a brother or sister is in error, we should be praying for them. If their ministry is attacked by the world through law suits or other means, we should be upholding them and standing with them, and even offering practical support where possible. We are supposed to be on the same side in this battle! Why should we go and join the ranks of the enemy to fight against our brothers and sisters, just because we disagree with them?

To publicly tear down another minister or ministry destroys the unity of the Body. Jesus' great high-priestly prayer before His death was that His followers should be one. The lack of unity in the Body of Christ has been one of the greatest stumbling blocks to many finding the Kingdom of God. Jesus did not establish thousands of churches, He established one Church. That Church is meant to stand as one man, and as one man to come to the "stature of the fullness of Christ", so that the world may see Jesus. How can that happen if parts of the body are continually trying to tear down other parts, and rejoicing to see their downfall when it happens? If a person's physical body is trying to destroy other parts of the body, it is called an auto-immune disease. These diseases are things such as multiple sclerosis, and can cause the body serious disablement and even death. The effect on the Body of Christ is no less devastating.

To publicly tear down another minister or ministry is to give room for the attack of the enemy, not only against the ministry we are tearing down but against the Body of Christ as a whole. In a physical auto-immune disease, the body's defense system treats the body itself as an enemy, and attacks it as though it were an invading disease. This often means that the body is so busy fighting itself that it is unable to muster its forces to fight when a real disease attacks it form outside. It is exactly the same in the Body of Christ. If parts of the Body are too busy attacking other parts, and those other parts are too busy defending themselves from the attack of the Body, then the Body as a whole is not ready to meet the attack of the enemy which comes from outside, and as a result is often left defeated and bleeding, when it should be rising up in victory.

Does that mean that we should never stand for right doctrine, that we should accept every teaching that comes, no matter how "off the planet" it may be? Not at all! Truth is important, particularly when error could lead people away from the Lord. However, we need to remember that we fight the error, not the person. We do not need to "name names". It is sufficient to point out the error and grant our listeners the intelligence to be able to recognize that error when they come across it. And we need to allow the Lord to correct error in us first. That "speck" of wrong doctrine in our own hearts and minds may be just the thing which is preventing us from clearly seeing to remove the "log" from our brother's understanding.

Does it mean that we should condone wrong behaviour, even if it causes great pain and distress to other people? Not at all! Those who have been wronged need to see justice. However, we need to stand in love with our brothers and sisters, even when they are in the wrong, and pray that the Lord would bring them through and restore them. After all, where would we have been if Jesus had refused to stand with us in the times when we caused pain and distress to others?

We need to teach the truth. We will never be able to counter every false doctrine in the world, and if we tried to we would only create confusion in our own minds and in the minds of our listeners. Teach the truth, grounded in the Word, with a heart that is open to God's correction. If you do that well, you will never need to worry about your listeners being led astray by false teachings, because they will have the truth as a standard by which all things can be measured.

As for individuals or ministries which teach wrongly, or who live in a way which does not reflect the Gospel, pray for them. Love them as Jesus loved you. Do all that you can to maintain the unity of the Body, and stand with them to fight against the enemy rather than standing with the enemy to fight against your brothers and sisters.

IS CHRISTMAS PAGAN?

Every Christmas and every Easter they come out of the woodwork: the well-intentioned Christian zealots shouting, "You can't celebrate that! It's pagan!"

So let's begin by acknowledging that, yes, there were at various times pagan rites celebrated at the times when we now celebrate the birth and the death of our Saviour. Does that mean that we should forego these celebrations and hand these times over to the devil?

Last Easter I read a comment from one Christian writer (can't remember now who it was) to the effect that "what has previously belonged to Satan cannot be redeemed." Now if that were true, then none of us would have any hope, for before we came to Jesus every one of us belonged to Satan. Praise God, Jesus' sacrifice has bought us back (redeemed) us out of that bondage. Can that redemption also be applied to times and celebrations? I believe it can, and that there is a Scriptural precedent for doing so.

In Judges 6:25-26 the Angel of the Lord tells Gideon to tear down his father's altar to Baal, and in its place to build an altar to the Lord, and to cut down the grove that was beside the altar and was also part of its pagan worship, and use the wood to offer his father's second bull as a sacrifice to the Lord. Note that this was not something that Gideon did out of his own understanding – in fact he was so fearful of the consequences from his family and the rest of the clan that he did it at night. This was specifically commanded by the Angel of the Lord (generally understood to be a pre-incarnate appearance of Christ): he was to take that which had been used in pagan worship and "redeem" it by using it to offer sacrifice to the

Lord.

Coming into the New Testament, in Acts 17:23 Paul is in Athens and comes upon an altar dedicated to An Unknown God. He immediately seizes upon this and says, "This God who is unknown to you, I will declare to you." There can be no doubt that in the thinking of the Athenians, the "Unknown God" was definitely a pagan deity. They might not have known which one, and probably thought it was simply best to cover their backs just in case there was one they had missed, but whoever or whatever it was, they definitely saw it as pagan. Yet Paul had no hesitation in picking up that which had belonged to Satan and commandeering it for the Kingdom of God. He may not have had a specific direction to do so, as Gideon had, but we can be confident that Paul walked closely enough with the Holy Spirit to be led by Him in this as in all his ministry.

So here we have two clear instances, one from the Old Testament and one from the New, where something which had belonged to Satan is redeemed to be used for the glory of God. Why should Christmas and Easter not be the same?

For me, the important question is not, "What did some other people hundreds or thousands of years ago celebrate at this time?" but, "What do I celebrate at this time?" Let me illustrate: I'm sure that over the millennia there have been thousands, probably millions, of people born on the same day as me. There have also been all kinds of events that have happened on that day, some good and some bad. Do I celebrate any of those things on my birthday? No, I celebrate my birthday. Likewise, when I celebrate Christmas, I do not celebrate Saturnalia or some other pagan festival, but the fact that God became Man, and was born in Bethlehem as a baby who grew up to live a perfect human life and die a cruel death bearing the sin of all mankind, and rose again in victory.

But what about Christmas trees? Doesn't Jeremiah 10:3-4 say that they are idols? Well, actually, no. Jeremiah was written hundreds of years before Jesus was born. Christmas didn't even exist then, so how could it be talking about Christmas trees? Jeremiah was talking to his own generation, speaking against those who cut down trees which they fashioned into idols. It's unfortunate that the KJV uses the word "deck", the same word used for decorating a Christmas tree, but in this case it meant covering it with silver or gold to make it beautiful.

Christmas trees are actually a very Christian tradition which originated in Europe in the middle ages. Conscious of the fact that there was no room in the inn for Jesus, in winter Christians would place lights in trees outside their homes to say to travellers, "There is room for you here. You can be safe and warm." Later they added decorations so that the trees would also be noticeable during the day. Then, because then as now there were some unscrupulous characters who would steal these lights or decorations, they began bringing the trees inside and setting them up in a window to show that hospitality was available.

So we have a choice: we can do the "holier than thou" thing, declare Christmas a pagan celebration, and hand it over to Satan. Or we can shout joyfully, "Jesus is the Reason for the Season" and rejoice in the fact that this is a time of the year when even unbelievers turn their minds to the Saviour. Which do you think God would prefer?

EIGHT REASONS TO PRAISE THE LORD

Ps.92

"It is good to praise the Lord" declares the Psalmist. We would agree, but I sometimes wonder whether our praise is really intelligent praise or simply the mouthing of words. "Praise the Lord" "Hallelujah" "Bless God" – the familiar phrases can become like a mantra, uttered by our lips while our minds are in neutral! Intelligent praise, on the other hand, has a reason behind it, and in this psalm the psalmist gives us eight good reasons.

1. Verse 2. His love and faithfulness. Where would we be without it? It was only because of His love that He created us at all. Looking out before creation at a world which would rebel and reject Him, He could just as easily have said, "This lot are going to be too much trouble. Forget it! I'm happy the way I am." Instead, He not only created us but then gave His very best in the person of Jesus Christ to bring us back to Himself. Through all our ups and downs, all our falling away and coming back, He is there, faithful and loving.

2. Verse 4. His creation. I once read a story about a doctor who had on his desk a wonderful, intricate piece of sculpture. Beautifully crafted, with wheels balanced within wheels, it attracted great admiration. One day a man whom the doctor knew to be an evolutionist came for a consultation. He was fascinated with the sculpture, and asked the doctor who had made it. "Oh, no-one made it," the doctor replied. "It just all came together by chance over a long period of time."

God's creation is far more wonderful, intricate and beautiful than any sculpture. It stretches from the incredible detail of the atom to the unimaginable vastness of the universe, and even the smallest piece of it contains complexities which boggle our minds. Truly, "When I consider the heavens, the work of Your hands, the moon and stars which You have set in place, what is man that You are mindful of him…"

3. Verse 7. The ultimate triumph of justice. "It's not fair!" How often parents have heard that from little Sally or Sam, as she or he stamped away, bottom lip dragging on the ground. The truth is, life isn't fair. All of us could name any number of situations in which the bad guy wins, the government takes from the poor and gives to the rich, the justice system defends the crooks and punishes the victims, and the person who tries to do the right thing gets kicked in the teeth for his efforts. The world is like that because of sin – not just the individual sin of the people involved, but the sin principle working in the world's systems to drag them into corruption. Those of us who have a heart for God struggle to find a balance between the need to accept a certain amount of injustice as inevitable (or else go insane thinking about it) and the need to resist injustice where we can make a difference. The day is coming, though, when those struggles will be over. Evil and injustice will finally be dealt with, and Jesus Christ will reign in righteousness. It's not just "pie in the sky", it's the future hope that makes the present struggle worthwhile.

4. Verse 10. The anointing of God. In the Old Testament days the anointing was only for prophets, priests and kings, but under the New Covenant it is for every believer. It isn't just the preacher or the song leader or the missionary who has the anointing – every believer does! What's more, the anointing isn't just a "force" or a "thing", but a person – the person of the Holy Spirit, who comes to dwell within every believer when they are born again. With God's anointing comes God's ability for whatever He may ask us to do. Every one of us has

a special place in the Body of Christ, a special task that only we can do – and the anointing means we already have all we need to do it!

5. Verse 11. Personal Victory. Many people who don't know the Bible well think the Psalms are all sweetness and light, lovey-dovey and praise the Lord! In fact, many of them are far from it! Some reflect the deepest pits of the writer's experience (try Ps 88 for sheer depression!) and others call loud and strong for the judgement and destruction of the psalmist's enemies (it is a bit hard to see love and peace, for example, in Ps 137:8-9). In this psalm, even though he doesn't use anything like the force of the "imprecatory psalms", the writer still looks to God for victory over his personal enemies. This side of the cross we see our human enemies in different terms (or at least we should). However, there are still many enemies over which we want victory – sin, bad habits, sickness, poverty, defeat… the list goes on. The good news, and certainly a very good reason to praise God, is that in Jesus Christ that victory is available to us.

6. Verses 12-13. The blessings of the righteous. No, the Christian life isn't a bed of roses, and no, your problems don't all disappear in a puff of smoke the moment you accept Jesus – in fact sometimes they get worse. We are still stuck in that old corrupt and unfair world system, and will suffer the affects just like anyone else. In Jer 45, the Lord sternly rebukes His servant Baruch for wanting to be treated better than the rest of the people. Nevertheless, no matter how difficult things might get, the Christian life is a life of blessing which the world will never understand. The peace and joy of the Holy Spirit are riches which cannot be measured.

7. Verse 14. Longevity of service. I re-entered the workforce in my mid-40s, having been out of secular employment for nearly 20 years. By and large, the commercial world didn't want to

know about me – I was "over 40 and over the hill". Our society pensions people off at 60 or 65, and after that they are seen as having no value to society. Praise God, He's different! As someone once said, "In God you are never retired, only re-fired!" He has a purpose for every one of us, and He won't take us home till that purpose is fulfilled. That means, if you are still on planet earth, then whether you're 10 or 110, you still have work to do for God.

8. Verse 15. God's strength and security. The Bible often describes God as a rock. Strong. Solid. Dependable. Unmovable. These are things we need in a world where the only certainty is change. Just look at the progress of information technology. When I was at school, computers were mysterious machines that whirred and clanked and took up whole rooms. It was inconceivable that I would ever even be close to one. Now I have one sitting on my desk (though it does still whir and clank at times!) I read recently that there is more computer power in a musical greeting card than there was in the whole world before 1950, and more computer power under the bonnet of a modern car than there was in the first rocket to the moon! Thirty years ago the rate of change in our world was described as Future Shock. Today, Future Shock is present tense. In the midst of it all, how good to know that our God is a rock, unmoving and unchanging.

So there we have it – eight good, intelligent reasons to praise the Lord. I'm sure with very little effort you can find a lot more.

WHAT SHOULD THE PROPHETS SPEAK?

Some time ago I heard statements from two men, both of whom have my deepest admiration and respect, but who take widely divergent views on this matter.

The first is a friend of mine in the USA: a prophet of the old school, hard-hitting, pull-no-punches and in your face. He takes the view that no prophet has the right to ever prophecy about God's love and goodness. People don't need to hear that, he says, they need to be called to repentance and commitment and set on fire for God. Particularly prophets should not talk about God as "Daddy" - He is the God of might and power and judgement.

Now let me be very clear that I have absolutely no doubt about my friend's prophetic call and anointing. I am one of the people who have been prodding him to accept it and publicly acknowledge it. However, I also recognise that we are all products of our history as well as of the working of God in our lives, and my friend's history includes a father who was cruel and distant, and a life of hardship struggling to survive. I am sure that at least some of his understanding of God is seen through those coloured glasses.

At the other end of the scale is a pastor whom I have never met, but whose ministry through the internet has blessed me enormously. The leader of a huge church in the USA, he regularly sees incredible healings and miracles released, not only through his own ministry, but through the ordinary people in his church, who are encouraged in their daily lives to look out for people who may be in need of a touch from God, and to pray for them. The result has been impromptu healing meetings in supermarkets, cafes and even on a trans-Atlantic flight!

I love this man's ministry, because so much of it is parallel to the vision that the Lord has given us for the ministry I lead. However, there is one point where I disagree (at least, the only one I have found so far) and that is his insistence that prophets should only ever speak good things. His reasoning is that the Word tells us that we prophesy according to our faith, and it takes far more faith to prophesy good outcomes than bad.

Much as I admire and respect both of them, I believe both these brothers miss the point. Very simply, if we are truly moving in the prophetic, God does not give us the option of choosing what we will say. Yes, the Word tells us that the spirit of the prophets is subject to the prophets, but that is concerning the timing and manner of delivery of the message, not the subject and content of the message. Prophecy is not about man giving man's opinion. It is about God speaking to His people through a vessel who is totally yielded to Him and prepared to deliver His message, regardless of whether the prophet himself likes the message or not.

Often in Scripture the message was a hard one, precisely because the time when God needed to send the prophets was generally the time when His people were not listening to what they already had, His written Word in the Law. The role of the prophet has changed somewhat under the New Covenant, because the people of God now have the Holy Spirit living within, and we are supposed to be led and directed by Him, not by God speaking through someone else. However, just as it was true that the people of Israel often ignored what they had (the Law), so it is true that Christians often ignore the Spirit. When we do, God sends His prophets, and we can expect their words to be sharp and to the point (enter my friend!) There are times when, as much as God wants to tell us of His love, He has to warn us of His judgement to shake us out of our complacency.

On the other hand, prophecy in the New Covenant also has another dimension: edification, exhortation and comfort. It might be said that, if we were walking perfectly in the Christian life as it is available to us, external edification, exhortation and comfort should not be needed, because all would be supplied by the indwelling Holy Spirit. But then, at the end of the temptation in the wilderness, God sent angels to comfort Jesus - and there has never been a person who walked more fully in the Spirit than He did. In any case, I have yet to meet anyone who walks perfectly in the Christian life as it is available to us, so this role for prophecy is valid for us all. There are times for all of us when we need confirmation that what we believe we have heard from God is right. Times when we need His reassurance that we are on the right track. And, yes, times when we simply need to hear Him say, "I love you. I am pleased with you."

From a human viewpoint, we can't always know where someone else is at. We might well perceive someone as needing a sharp rebuke, when what they really need is to hear God's acceptance and affirmation. Or we might want to say, "God loves you", when they really need "Wake up and turn around, before God has to discipline you severely."

That's why prophecy must have its source in the heart and mind of God. He alone knows the depths of people's lives. If we limit ourselves to only bringing prophecies of rebuke and judgement, we may miss giving someone the word of hope that could turn his life around. If we bring only prophecies of goodness and light, we may fail to issue the warning that could save a soul - or a nation - from destruction.

EXTRAVAGANT LOVE

- A Tale of Two Women

In the Gospels we find the stories of two women who, in the external circumstances of their lives, were very different, but who had the same heart. The first is found in Luke 7:36-50, the second in the other 3 Gospels – Matt 26: 6-13, Mark 14:3-9 and John 12:1-8. Many people think that all four accounts refer to the same woman, so first we need to establish the differences.

Luke's story takes place early in Jesus' ministry, in the home of a Pharisee. The lack of common courtesy which he demonstrated toward Jesus clearly indicates that the sole purpose in inviting Him was to try to find a way to trap Him in His words. The other guests were obviously not followers of Jesus, for His followers would hardly have been so surprised about His forgiveness of the woman. Undoubtedly they were other Pharisees, also seeking to catch Jesus out.

The woman comes on the scene as a total intruder. Most certainly she was not invited! It is extremely doubtful that any of those present knew her personally – although they all definitely knew of her by reputation, and some may quite possibly have made use of her services.

She is described as a "sinner". This means that she was either a prostitute or a "loose" woman. She was an outcast in society. Except for Jesus, every person in the room that day, had he met her on the street, would have crossed to the other side of the road rather than risk contamination by coming near her.

Well aware of who she is, she comes humbly and broken, and stands behind Him, pouring her perfume on His feet and wiping them with her hair.

Jesus is condemned in the mind of His hosts for letting this "sinner" touch Him. He in turn condemns His host, both for his lack of hospitality and for his failure to understand the principles of repentance and forgiveness.

The other accounts take place right at the end of Jesus' ministry, just before He is to go to the Cross. The situation is very different. Even though the host has the same name, Simon, this is a co-incidence – consider that at one time Simon Peter stayed with Simon the Tanner, and you realize how common a name Simon was. This Simon, however, was not a Pharisee, but one of the disciples. Jesus was an honoured guest, along with Martha and Mary and their brother Lazarus, whom Jesus had raised from the dead. The context seems to suggest that it was a kind of testimony meeting, a time for Lazarus to share his experience and to honour Jesus for the miracle.

The woman, Mary of Bethany, is certainly not an intruder on this scene, but one specially invited to share in the celebrations.

Far from being a loose woman, she is a highly respected member of the community, and highly regarded among the disciples as one of Jesus' closest personal friends. No stranger, she is well known by all those present.

Perhaps emulating the first woman, whose story she had undoubtedly heard, in John's account she pours the perfume on Jesus feet and wipes them with her hair. Thus she indicates that she recognizes that she, too, is a sinner who needs Jesus' forgiveness. Then, however, as recorded in Matthew and

Mark, she pours the perfume on His head, showing that she understood that He had brought her into a relationship of intimacy which qualified her to "anoint Him for burial".

She (and by implication, Jesus) is condemned for the waste of money, but Jesus commends her for her demonstration of devotion – and by implication condemns the rest of the disciples for their lack of devotion.

Two very different situations, two very different women, yet both demonstrated a heart that put to shame those around them.

Both demonstrated a love that was reckless. The first woman broke into a situation where she knew she was unwelcome, where she knew she would be condemned, belittled and looked down upon. She was prepared to face all that, to take hold of the grace that she knew would flow from Jesus, if only she could get to Him.

Mary, who could have remained comfortable in her respectability, chose to behave in a manner which was most unacceptable in her middle class circle, knowing full well that such behaviour would bring ridicule and condemnation, and may well damage her standing in society. She was prepared to risk her reputation, for no better reason than to demonstrate her love for Jesus.

Both demonstrated a love that was extravagant. Both brought the very best they could lay their hands on, and shattered it at the feet of the Lord. There was no holding back, no sense that this was a waste of money, no substitution of something less. It is impossible to read these accounts without having a sense that, for both women, the material offering of the alabaster jar and its contents was but a symbol of their entire lives, poured as an offering to Jesus.

Both demonstrated a love that was intuitive and full of faith. The first woman was so sure that Jesus would forgive her, that she poured out her thankfulness for that forgiveness even before she received it. Mary, apparently the only one among the disciples who had actually heard and believed Jesus' words about His impending death, saw beyond that death to resurrection, and was so able to prepare His body for the grave. Can you imagine how impossible that would have been if she had thought that His death was going to be the end?

What about us? How much are we willing to risk for Jesus? How much are we prepared to lavish upon Him?

HIS WORD ABOVE HIS NAME

Psa 138:2 I will worship toward thy holy temple, and praise thy name for thy lovingkindness and for thy truth: for thou hast magnified thy word above all thy name. (KJV)

In my prayer time this morning the Holy Spirit gave me a real revelation about this verse, which has always been a puzzling one to me, and I would like to share it with you. The second part of the verse, "Thou hast magnified Thy word above all Thy Name," was mentioned in the service at church on Sunday, and I had been meditating on it since.

What the Lord showed me ties in with a promise and a warning.

The promise is Jesus' words in John 14:13 "And whatsoever ye shall ask in my name, that will I do, that the Father may be glorified in the Son."(KJV) This is repeated in slightly different format in John 15:16 "Ye have not chosen me, but I have chosen you, and ordained you, that ye should go and bring forth fruit, and that your fruit should remain: that whatsoever ye shall ask of the Father in my name, he may give it you" (KJV) and again in John 16:23 "And in that day ye shall ask me nothing. Verily, verily, I say unto you, Whatsoever ye shall ask the Father in my name, he will give it you."(KJV)

In each of these verses, Jesus tells us that His Name gives us the authority to ask for whatever we want, and God will honour the authority of Jesus' Name and give us our request.

So, does that mean that you can ask in Jesus' Name for your best friend's husband to leave her and marry you? Absolutely not! But didn't Jesus say we could ask for ANYTHING in His Name? Yes, He did, but the Word of God says "You shall not commit adultery." The Word outweighs the Name. We can use the Name of Jesus till we turn blue, but if what we are asking for does not line up with the Word, then it will not happen, because God will always honour His Word above His Name.

The warning relates to Jesus words in Mat 7:21-23 "Not every one that saith unto me, Lord, Lord, shall enter into the kingdom of heaven; but he that doeth the will of my Father which is in heaven.

Many will say to me in that day, Lord, Lord, have we not prophesied in thy name? and in thy name have cast out devils? and in thy name done many wonderful works? And then will I profess unto them, I never knew you: depart from me, ye that work iniquity." (KJV) Sadly, many things are done "in the Name of Jesus" that simply do not line up with the Word of God. In recent days I have seen two posts on social media that highlight this. One was an article about a church in the USA that has hired a psychic medium as part of its ministry team. The other was an ad for a "Christian Witches Convention." These things are being done in Jesus' Name, so doesn't that make them ok? Again, absolutely not! In both cases, these run directly counter to God's Word in Deuteronomy 18:9-12, which lists the occult practices and declares that those who do such things are an abomination to God. We cannot paste Jesus' Name onto something that is against His Word, because He will honour His Word over His Name every time.

These examples are, of course, the extreme, but the principle applies across the board: if we try to put His Name on that which His Word forbids, He will not honour it or us. What's more, we may find ourselves guilty of taking His Name in vain - using it for a purpose for which it was not intended.

Jesus has given us the authority of His Name, both for our prayers and for our service, but we must always be sure to use His Name in a way that lines up with His Word.

FAITH AND FIRE

A Short Story

I stood looking up at it. Towering ninety feet above the plain, its glistening gold seeming to capture the fire of the sun, it was easily the most noticeable thing for miles around. Nebuchadnezzar had certainly got everyone's attention with this one!

Of course, we had been hearing the rumours for weeks. I couldn't help wondering whether maybe it had something to do with the dream. Some time before, the king had dreamed of a great statue. In fact, we very nearly all lost our heads over that dream, because none of the wise men was able to tell the king what he had dreamed, or to give him the interpretation. He was so angry that he ordered all the wise men in the kingdom to be killed - including us! Fortunately, when Daniel learned of the situation he cried out to our God, the God of Heaven, and He graciously gave Daniel the answer for the king and saved all our lives.

For me, that was the beginning of my feeling that God was real, and that He was truly with us in this place. Before that, to be honest, I was none to sure. Back in the land of Judah we had heard many of our elders scoffing at the prophets, those crazy men who wandered around doing all manner of ridiculous things, and all the while declaring doom and gloom everywhere. Didn't they know that we were God's chosen people? That we were from the tribe of the great Kind David? How could they imagine that He would allow any other nation to have victory over us? No wonder the elders laughed!

Yet it happened just as the prophets had said. Babylon attacked and defeated us, and we were carried off as exiles to the land of the Babylonians. Some of my friends - Daniel, Mishael and Azaria - and I, Hananiah, somehow ended up in the royal court. We were only young men. Each of us had seen only sixteen or seventeen summers. And yet, here we were, training to be part of the civil service in a foreign country.

It may sound glamorous, but it was far from easy. First there was the language, then a whole set of new manners and customs to learn. I ached for my homeland, for the familiar sounds, for the sight of the Temple and the priests in their robes, for the comforting knowledge that we as a people had a special relationship with God. That He was on our side.

All that was gone now. It was as if God had turned His back on us. The Babylonians even took away our names, all of which included a reference to the Lord, and named us instead after their own false gods. Instead of being "the Lord shows grace" I became Shadrach, "command of Aku." Mishael, "Who is what God is?" became Meshach, "Who is what Aku is?" and Azaria, whose name meant "The Lord helps" was called Abednego, "Servant of Nego." Daniel's name meant "God is my judge". The Babylonians called him Belteshazzar, meaning "Bel protects his life", but somehow in spite of it, Daniel always remained Daniel. He was the strongest of the four of us. I imagine in two thousand years' time, Daniel will still be Daniel and we three will be Shadrach, Meshach and Abednego! (Who am I kidding? Who will remember four Hebrew boys even twenty years after we have gone, much less two thousand?)

Over all, it was pretty depressing, even though the four of us were rising quickly through the ranks of the Babylonian civil service. I for one would happily have given up our new-found status to be back home where God was real and faith was easy.

Then the king had that dream, and God gave Daniel the interpretation, and suddenly it began to all make sense. Not only did God show that He was real, and that He cared about us, but I began to feel that maybe there was a bigger purpose in us being here. Certainly the whole thing shook up Nebuchadnezzar, to the point where he declared, "Surely your God is the God of gods and the Lord of kings!" That's a pretty big statement from a gentile idol worshipper.

But I have digressed. As I said, I couldn't help wondering whether this statue was a result of the statue in the king's dream. The dream statue had a golden head, which represented Nebuchadnezzar. Its chest and arms of silver represented another, lesser kingdom that would replace his, and the belly and thighs of bronze a further, still lesser kingdom that would replace it. Its legs of iron and feet of iron mixed with clay were a fourth, inferior kingdom. Finally, a rock cut out by non-human hands smashed the whole thing, breaking it to pieces and establishing a kingdom that will last for ever.

Was this huge, golden statue that now dominated the plain of Dura Nebuchadnezzar's attempt to say that all those lesser kingdoms would not replace him, but that his kingdom, the golden kingdom, would stand forever?

My thoughts were interrupted by a trumpet blast, and the loud cry of a herald, and I quickly realised that I had far more to worry about than trying to analyse the king's motives.

When all the musical instruments sounded, the herald declared, everyone was to bow down and worship this statue. Those who refused would be thrown into a blazing furnace.

A cold shudder ran down my back. I looked around at my companions, Mishael and Azaria, and could tell at once from their faces that they were every bit as stunned as I was. Had it really come to this? Our faith had been stretched to breaking point already, was it now to be tested beyond our ability?

Not a word passed between us as we gazed from one to another, searching each other's eyes for a response. Slowly, deliberately, an almost imperceptible shake of the head from each. Another look, and an equally deliberate, barely discernible nod. We all knew where we stood, and we stood together.

The music sounded: horns, flutes, zithers, lyres, harps - a cacophony of every kind of instrument. Around us everyone dropped whatever they were doing and fell down to worship the statue. We stood. Silently, we prayed. We knew our God was able to deliver us from whatever fate lay before us. Swallowing our fear, we chose to believe that He would. Could we know for sure? We knew that none of us was certain, but we also knew that no matter what the outcome, we could not bow. The honour of our God was more important than our lives. Live or die, we would not - could not - deny Him.

Of course, there were those who were quick to denounce us, all too pleased that they now had both an excuse and a means to get rid of us. We were hauled before the king, and he was furious. His earlier acknowledgement of our God had vanished, and he demanded us to worship his false gods or face the furnace.

It's funny, how a crisis clarifies and focuses your thoughts. In that moment, standing before the king who had all the earthly power in the world, including that of life or death, a strange calm settled over us. Every doubt that we had ever had about God's reality vanished, replaced with a knowing that was more certain than certainty. Fear fled, and we stood as if clothed with an authority far beyond that of the king. We still did not know that God would rescue us, but we knew that we were in

His hands, and even in death nothing could touch us but what He allowed.

We spoke with one voice. "Our God is able to save us from your furnace, and He will do so. But even if He doesn't, we will not bow to your false gods."

The whole thing takes on a dream-like quality from that point on. The king was shouting, the courtiers were shouting, the soldiers were shouting. They quickly shovelled more fuel onto the fire, heating the furnace to seven times its normal level. Almost before we could blink, we were grabbed and bundled quickly from arm to arm up the human chain that led to the mouth of the furnace. Soldiers dragged us the last part of the way, but the heat was such that they collapsed and died even as they pushed us into the flames.

There was no time for us to think or to feel fear or anything else. Before we knew it we were standing in the middle of the fire. Then it hit us. We were standing in the middle of the fire! I looked around. Yes, there was Mishael, and Azaria. Each one looked perfectly normal, not bothered at all by the heat. They weren't even sweating! Neither was I!

Then I looked up, and standing in the midst of us was Another. The warmth and power that emanated from Him made the fire seem lifeless. An overwhelming flood of worship engulfed my being, and I knew that our faith had met our God.

FAITHFUL SERVANTS

My Old Testament reading this morning took me again through the book of Daniel. When I came to Chapter 6, I was once again struck by the importance of being faithful in whatever God may set before us.

Most of us know the story of Daniel in the lions' den: we have heard it since we were in Sunday School. But do you know the background to the story?

For a start, Daniel was not a young boy as many retellings of the story present him. He had been taken to Babylon under Nebuchadnezzar, in 605 BC. The lions' den incident happened under the reign of Darius, who came to power in 539 BC. That means it was at least 66 years after Daniel arrived in Babylon. He was probably around 20 when he was transported, which means that at the time of this event he was 86 years old!

For almost the whole of those 66 years, he had distinguished himself in the civil service of a foreign country. He was one of the major prophets of the Bible, but he was not a professional minister, paid by the faithful, but an employee of a series of heathen kings.

For all those years, he had been one of the highest-ranking civil servants in the land, and at the beginning of Chapter 6 we find that King Darius is so impressed with him that he is about to set him over the whole kingdom as second-in-command under himself, just as Pharaoh had done many years before with the young Joseph.

Not surprisingly, this aroused some jealousy in the other

members of the civil service, many of whom were no doubt considerably younger than Daniel and wondered why such an old man should be kept on at all. So, they set out to "dig some dirt" on him, to find some basis of accusation by which they could expose him to Darius and keep him out of the top position.

Now, in almost any governmental structure in the world, at almost any time in history, and in relation to almost any individual, this should have been a very easy thing to do. The despotic systems of the ancient world particularly lent them selves to corruption (as do such systems today); bribery was a common way of life, nepotism was rampant and neglect of duties was the done thing.

Yet no matter how hard they searched, they could not find any dirt on Daniel. The Scripture says he was neither corrupt nor negligent. In 66 years of service, there was not one thing that Daniel had done or failed to do that could be used against him. What a record!

It was only after this abysmal failure to find any fault in Daniel's work that they decided to use his faith to trap him. Appealing to Darius's pride, and leaning on the fact that once the king passed a law it could not be repealed, they persuaded Darius to pass a decree that, for the next month, no-one should pray to any god except him.

When Daniel continued to pray openly to YHWH, not even the king - now realising his foolishness - could save him from the lions' den. God, however, was not yet finished with Daniel. He sent His angel to close the lion's mouths, and Daniel was delivered unscathed, whilst those who had sought his downfall were sent to the fate they had intended for him.

Daniel was faithful in every area of his life. He was faithful in his personal devotion to YHWH, not only refusing to give up worship (how many of us would have been tempted to say, "Oh well, it's only for a month"?), but refusing even to hide the fact that he was worshipping YHWH (how many of us would have thought, "I don't **have to** pray on the rooftop. I'll just hide in the closet for this month"?)

He had been faithful all his life in the discharge of his ministry, speaking into the lives of kings and nations with the same kind of boldness.

He had also been faithful in his secular work. He had resisted the temptations of shortcuts and easy money, and had proved himself to be of the highest value to his masters, the kings of Babylon. He did not see his work as less important than the ministry, therefore worthy of less attention and care, but gave himself fully and faithfully to the task at hand. That very faithfulness opened the door for him to bring the Word of the Lord to kings and nations, and to us today. That faithfulness also put him in the position to receive a miracle so outstanding that it is still talked about today, two-and-a-half thousand years later.

What has God placed before you? Are you faithful in it?

TWO MALIGNED BIBLE WOMEN

There are two women in the New Testament who are regularly mis-judged by Christians.

The first is the Samaritan woman with whom Jesus talked at the well. Many Christians assume that she had been divorced five times, but Jesus did not say that. He said only that she had had five husbands. It is just as possible that she had been widowed five times. In fact, given the culture of the day, and particularly the fact that many women married men who were considerably older than themselves, that is probably a more likely scenario. It also could explain why "the one you are with now is not your husband." I can just imagine the conversation from the man she was with: "Live with me. I will care for you and provide for you. But every man that has been married to you has died. I don't want to take that chance."

Jesus' words to this lady were not a condemnation, but an offer of understanding and acceptance.

The second mis-judged woman is Mary Magdalene, whom many consider to have been a prostitute. There is absolutely nothing in the Bible to suggest this was the case. The only New Testament reference to Mary's past is that Jesus had cast seven demons out of her (Mar 16:9, Lk 8:2) but there is no indication of what these demons might have been.

The problem arises because people identify Mary with the woman who anointed Jesus' feet in Luke 26-36, but there is no reason to see this woman as Mary.

This confusion can be avoided when we understand that there were two incidents in which a woman anointed Jesus. Let's compare them:

The first, recorded in Luke, occurred at the beginning of Jesus' ministry; the second, recorded in Mk 14:3-9, Matt 26:6-13 and John 12:1-8, occurred right at the end of his ministry.

The woman in the first was an unnamed sinner (probably a prostitute); the woman in the second was Mary of Bethany (NOT Mary Magdalene), sister of Martha and Lazarus, a disciple and a woman of standing in her community.

The first took place in the home of a Pharisee, who had undoubtedly invited Jesus in the hope of trapping Him in something He said. In this home Jesus was accorded no honour, not even the common courtesies that were expected to be given to any guest. The second took place in the home of a man known as Simon the Leper (who had obviously been healed, otherwise he would not have been able to live in the town and have guests at his home) and seems to have been a celebration of Jesus raising Lazarus and possibly healing Simon. In this home Jesus was accorded great honour. (Yes, both hosts were named Simon. But when you know that at one point in the book of Acts Simon Peter was staying in the home of Simon the Tanner, they you realise what a common name Simon was.)

In the first instance, Jesus was rebuked for allowing a sinful woman to touch Him. In the second instance, Mary was rebuked for "wasting" the ointment she poured on Jesus.

In the first instance, the woman was responding in faith and love to the forgiveness she had found in Jesus. In the second, Mary was responding in grief because she understood what Jesus had been telling them about His upcoming death (when none of the male disciples seem to have "got it".)

These are obviously two separate incidents, and Mary Magdalene is not involved in either. (If you think it unlikely that there would be two similar incidents in Jesus' life, consider this: two incidents of Jesus feeding thousands with a few loaves and fish are recorded just a chapter apart in Matthew. There were also two incidents of a miraculous catch of fish, one at the beginning of Jesus' ministry and one at the end.)

Please stop maligning Mary Magdalene and the Samaritan woman. Neither of them deserves the reputation that the church has given them.

BEYOND IMAGINATION

Imagine the cost:
heaven's perfection forsaken,
earth's corruption embraced;
infinity reduced
to a single cell;
omnipotence exchanged
for impotence;
omniscience buried
in ignorance.

Imagine the ache:
to walk in a world
that sees not,
nor cares;
revelation met
with rejection
and miracles
with scorn;
offering the eternal
to those who
only want a feed.

Imagine the agony:
flesh rent
stripped from bone;
nerves and tendons
cleft by spikes;
heart crushed.

Imagine the horror:
upon the sinless head
earth's sin-sewage

dumped;
the Father
turned away;
alone, forsaken.

Imagine the victory:
grave's doors
flung wide;
death's hold
shattered;
sin's power
forever smashed.

Imagine the wonder:
it was for me.

ARE YOU A DISCIPLE OR JUST A FAN?

Palm Sunday. On that long-ago day which we celebrate today, the "Jesus Fan Club" was out in force. These people had watched Jesus over the last few years, and had decided that He was just wonderful.

They had seen Him heal all manner of sicknesses with no more than a word, although sometimes He also touched the person or even did something strange like putting mud on a man's eyes. But no matter how He did it, He never failed! There was never a single person who went to Him looking for healing who did not get healed. He even raised the dead! People who were oppressed and possessed by demons, even the very worst of them, were set free.

He did other things, too, like feeding great multitudes with just a few fish and a couple of bread rolls, and turning several barrels of water into wine for a wedding party (most of them particularly liked that one!) He had authority over wind and storms, and nothing seemed too difficult for Him. He had authority when He spoke, too – He seemed to know what He was talking about, unlike all the other teachers they had known.

And yet He was such a nice, down-to-earth fellow. He talked about things they understood – fishing and farming, houses and ships and sheep – unlike the high-minded Pharisees with their long words and religious waffle. Best of all, they felt good when they were around Him – like they were accepted, approved, loved. Yes, this Jesus was just great!

Some of them had even began to drop His name in their

conversations: "When I was with Jesus the other day" (the fact that they were three-quarters of the way to the back in a crowd of nearly 10,000 was a minor detail.) Now, He was coming into Jerusalem, and someone had put forward the wonderful idea that they should make Him king! Just think, no-one would ever be sick or hungry again, fishermen would never again come home without a catch, and there would never be a lack of wine for parties. If ever anyone had a good election platform, it was Jesus.

So they went out to meet Him, shouting "Hosanna" and waving palm branches, throwing their cloaks on the road for Him to ride over, and each doing everything possible to be noticed by Him. They were riding high on a crest of adulation, and the object of their zeal could do no wrong.

How different it was just five days later, when this same man, having been betrayed by His friend and rushed through a mockery of a trial, stood before Pilate facing the death sentence. Offered the choice, this same "Fan Club" who would have made Jesus king now chose a murderer instead, and when asked what they wanted to do with this Christ their "Hosannas" changed to "Crucify! Crucify!"

The question is for each of us: are we disciples, or just fans? As then, there are many in the world today who are members of the "Jesus Fan Club". They think Jesus is great, particularly when He does good things in their lives such as healing or meeting some material need. They like the good feeling they get in a hyped-up church meeting where they sing loudly and dance around to show how much they love Him. They think it will be really good when He rules on earth and there is no more sorrow or pain or sickness or need.

The trouble is, fans are only there for the good times. When the hard times come, they change their loyalty to someone else. They will not stay when things get difficult.

Fans are only interested in "what's in it for me?" They have no real loyalty to the person, they are only staying around for what they can get.

Fans are not interested in a genuine relationship, which takes work and effort. They just want the second-hand glory of being linked, however tenuously, to someone great.

Disciples, however, have a commitment to a person. Whilst they will certainly enjoy the benefits that relationship brings, they want the relationship for itself, and even if the benefits were taken away they would still continue in the relationship. They want their lives to be genuinely changed by the relationship. Even if things get difficult, they will hold on, knowing that this is part of the discipline which discipleship is about.

Interesting and exciting times lie ahead for the Church. We are coming into a time when the Book of Acts will seem mild in comparison to the things God will do through His people. At the same time – in fact, as a direct result of this awesome move of God – the devil will rise up and begin to persecute God's people as never before.

In the times that lie ahead, the "Jesus Fan Club" will fall apart. Fans will not be able to stand either the responsibility and accountability which goes with God's outpouring or the persecution that comes as a result of it. Only true disciples, those who are with Jesus for the long time not just for the good time, will stand.

Before those times come, each one of us needs to honestly ask ourselves: "Am I a disciple, or just a fan?"

IS IT A <u>GOD</u> IDEA OR JUST A <u>GOOD</u> IDEA?

How many times have you planned to do something, only to find that no matter how hard you tried, it just didn't work out? How many times have you been busy doing any number of good things, but find that you don't have the time to do the things that are really on your heart? It is so easy, isn't it, to get caught up following plans and ideas, and at the end of the day wonder whether you really should have been doing something else entirely. As someone once said, some people can't see the forest for the trees, and some people can't see the trees for the forest, and some people are simply in the *wrong forest!*

As Christians, and particularly as ministers of the Gospel, we need to remember two things. Firstly, **the good is the enemy of the best.** I believe that often, when the devil finds that he cannot tempt us with evil, he will tempt us with good. That is, he will present us with are in themselves good, but which will keep us from God's best.

It is important for us to be able to distinguish between those things which are really of God, and those things which simply seemed like a good idea at the time. There are many good things which we could do, many good plans which we could make, but if they are not the things God would have us do, or the plans He would have us make, they are destined to failure. Psalm 127 tells us, "Unless the Lord builds the house, its builders labour in vain. Unless the Lord watches over the city, its watchmen stand guard in vain." Even when our "good" ideas appear to have some measure of success, that success will be limited unless they were "God" ideas.

Even more importantly, when we follow our own good ideas

(which are not God ideas), they can keep us from doing the things God really wants of us. Peter and the apostles faced this dilema in the days of the early church. In that culture, as in many places in the world today, the only "welfare system" was provided by the church. Widows, orphans and those in need looked to the church to provide them with food. Looking after these people was a good idea, and certainly one that God endorsed. However, it was not God's idea ***for the apostles.*** God had other work for them to do. But the demands of the feeding program were such that the apostles were finding themselves unable to take the time needed to prepare themselves for the work God had called them to, namely preaching the Gospel. Wisely, they asked the church to nominate suitable people to take over the work of managing the feeding program, and said "We will give ourselves to prayer and the ministry of the Word."

The second thing we need to remember, both for ourselves personally and for our ministries corporately, is that ***the need is not the call.*** There are many needs in the world, even in our own small corner of it, and none of us can answer all of them. If we try, we will very soon find ourselves at the point of breakdown. As individuals, we need to know what God's specific call is to us. Are you a pastor or an evangelist? They can be very different! Are you a teacher or an exhorter? A prophet or a counsellor? Whilst many people will have more than one gift or ministry, no one has them all. If I try to do what you are called to do, I will wear myself out because I am not you, and at the same time I will miss what I am called to. And vice versa.

Just as we as individuals each have a unique place in God's purposes, so our ministries also have a unique place. No one ministry is or can be all things to all people.

If you don't already know it, ask God to show you what your

inique call is. Ask Him also to show you His vision for your ministry. When you know God's purposes for your life and ministry, you will be much less likely to get caught up in good ideas whilst missing the God ideas. But don't leave it just with the "big picture". In each decision you make, take time to ask the Lord, "Is this Your idea, or just a good idea." Be like Jesus, who only did what He saw the Father doing and only said what He heard the Father saying.

GRATITUDE: THE POWER TO CHANGE LIVES

Thank you. It's one of the most powerful expressions in any human language. It tells the recipient that she is appreciated, that his effort is worthwhile, that she is valuable. It can lift the spirits of someone who has been having a bad day. It can re-energise the person who is just about on the point of giving up. It can overpower loneliness by making us feel that we have actually touched someone, and they us. It can turn drudgery into pleasure and tears into a song.

Yet for all its power toward the recipient, it is even more powerful for the giver. At the surface level, saying a sincere "thank you" for what someone has done for us, usually makes them want to do even more. People enjoy being appreciated so much - and, in many cases, receive so little of it - that they will go out of their way to get more. The key, of course, is that it must be sincere. Most people are very good at sniffing out phonies, and self-seeking thanks is likely to be rejected as the cynical exercise it is.

At a deeper level, being thankful does some important things in us, regardless of the response of the other person. For a start, it moves us out of the centre of the universe. It is so easy for us to become so ego-centric that we take everything that is done for us as a right. Yet often, in order for us to enjoy our perceived rights, someone else has to give up his. Unless you live alone and look after yourself, in order for you to enjoy a hot dinner someone had to give up her right to spend the afternoon watching television. For you to enjoy pleasant service at the supermarket, the checkout operator had to give up her right to carry the frustrations of the morning traffic through the day. The other person has feelings, needs and desires that get bruised, squashed and compromised when they come into contact with our needs. By thanking him for making the effort, we acknowledge him and take the focus off ourself - and that can be wonderfully liberating.

Secondly, it makes us aware of just how much we have for which we should be grateful. It's easy to focus on the negatives: sickness, bills, family disputes, and all the collected difficulties of life have a way of grabbing our attention and holding it. We then get bogged down in the blues, thinking about what we don't have. When we start thinking about the things in life for which we are grateful, we begin to see that the negatives aren't so overwhelming after all. Just the fact that we woke up this morning, that our hearts are beating and our lungs breathing, is a good start. Even if we are the poorest of the poor, and our relationships are few and terrible, there is so much in life that is free to everyone: the beauty of the sunset, the song of birds, the softness of an evening breeze. When we begin to look for those things, and to be grateful for them, we lift ourselves out of the negativity and begin to feel good about life again. We begin to move into contentment, not settling for what we have, but enjoying where we are as a stage in the process to where we are going.

I recently read something that suggested we even go beyond being grateful for the good things in life, and look for reasons to be thankful in the things we perceive as being bad. For instance, when your next phone bill comes in, rather than shuddering and wondering how you are going to pay it, take a moment to thank God for the technology that allows us to speak to people who are separated from us by huge physical distances. Just a couple of hundred years ago, the thought of being able to do such a thing would have been considered the wildest of fantasies!

Another interesting aspect of gratitude is that we tend to draw into our lives the things on which we focus most. If we are focused on debt, sickness and problems, then guess what we will get in greater abundance: debt, sickness and problems! When we focus on the positives by being grateful, we draw more of the positives to us.

Perhaps the most important aspect for us as Christians is that when we find a way to be thankful to God in whatever situation we find ourselves, we immediately remove that situation from the devil's hands. By being grateful to God we are acknowledging Him as being in control, and thus we cut off the power of the enemy to influence the outcome.

More than that, we can move gratitude into the future, being thankful for the answer that we know God will bring us. By doing this we are linking gratitude to our faith, thus strengthening our faith and placing ourselves in a position to receive from God.

With such great benefits coming from gratitude, it's amazing that we don't use it more. Take time today to sit down and write three lists. In the first, list the people who contribute to your life. Over the next few weeks, take the time to write each one a short thank you note. You will be amazed at their reactions.

In the second list, write down all the good things in your life for which you are grateful to God. Incorporate that list into your prayer time, taking the time to thank Him for all the things you have rather than just presenting a shopping list of the things you need.

In the third list, write all the negative, annoying things in your life, and find at least one thing about each for which you can be grateful. Focus on the positives, rather than the negatives.

Don't let this be just a one-off exercise that is then quickly forgotten, but revisit it regularly, building gratitude into your life as a habit. In twelve months time you may find that your life, and your level of enjoyment of it, is very different from what it is today.

HAS THE CLOUD MOVED?

Often we think of the forty years which Israel spent wandering in the wilderness as nothing but punishment for their sin of doubt and disobedience when they failed to cross the Jordan into the promised land, preferring to accept the negative reports of ten spies than the faith statements of the two. However, some very important things for the nation took place during those years, not the least of which was that they were forced to a place of total dependence upon God. Removed from any means by which they could provide for themselves, they had no choice but to look to God for everything they needed.

More than that, in their looking to God they had to be where He was. Day by day they had His visible presence with them in the pillar of cloud by day and the pillar of fire by night, reminding them that His provision and His protection could never be had apart from His presence. If any of them was silly enough to go charging off on his own, venturing out without the visible presence of God, he would very quickly find himself also removed from all the blessing that God's presence brought, and struggling to fend for himself. Likewise, if someone decided that he was comfortable where he was, and didn't want to move when the cloud began to move, he also would soon find that God's provision and protection were no longer with him. He could try as hard as he liked to take hold "by faith" of all that God was, and all that God wanted to be for him, but if he had removed himself from God's presence it simply was not going to happen.

We too need to learn to remain where the cloud is. Too often we want God's "presents" without His "presence". We forget that faith only works when it is pointed in the right direction.

Faith in faith will get us nowhere, and often faith in people will not get us much further. That doesn't me that we should not trust people, but people are not our source and never can be. Only God is our source (that's part of what it means for Him to be God) and only faith **in God** is effective faith. Faith, however, is a very immediate thing. It is not good at travelling long distances. If we are far from God's presence, faith simply doesn't work. We can strive and struggle and twist ourselves into all kinds of shapes trying to believe and to take hold of God's promises, but if we have removed ourselves from His presence, our faith has nothing to take hold of, and we find ourselves wondering what went wrong.

Our life with God is never static. It is always about moving, about growth, not about getting comfortable in one place (spiritually, and sometimes physically) and settling down. It is a "walk", not a "sit". (Yes, we are seated with Christ in heavenly places, but that is a different dimension.) Like the ancient Israelites, we need to learn to watch the cloud. We need to move when God moves, and to stand still when He stands still. We need to change our focus, so that the most important thing is not where we are, but where He is. When we focus on where we are, we start looking at our surroundings. Either they are very nice and we want to stay put – which becomes a problem when God wants to move – or they are anything but nice and we want to get out of there – which becomes a problem when God wants to stay put! When we focus on where He is, then that is where we want to be, regardless of what the circumstances surrounding us may be.

Are you finding that faith is a struggle and the blessing of God seems to have moved? Could it be that you have removed yourself from God's presence? Have you perhaps run ahead, eager to get on with the next thing, when God wants to linger where you have been, maybe to deal with some issues in your life, maybe to build deeper relationships, maybe simply to wait for His timing? Stop, step back, get back into God's presence. His timing will surely come, and when it does it will be perfect. More importantly, you will walk into His timing in His presence.

Others maybe have lingered behind when God was moving on. You have wanted to cling to what has been, to live in the old anointing. A friend of mine used to say, "God moves. Then man turns it into a movement, then he turns it into a monument, and finally he turns it into a mausoleum." Yesterday's anointing was wonderful – for yesterday. It was not made for tomorrow. That which is easy and comfortable may seem very nice, but it can lull us to sleep and desensitise us to both the presence of God and the danger of sin. If God has moved, then no matter how good yesterday was, you need to get up and leave it behind, and follow that cloud!

INCARNATE

Infinity
compressed to human skin
growing
where growth was
never needed.

Eternity
confined in time
moving
past present future
irreversible
when all points
had been now.

Omnipotence
reduced to weakness
helpless
dependent

Omnipresence
tied to three dimensions
locked
in the limitation
of finite space

Omniscience
embraces amnesia
a blank slate
for creation to write upon

The universe's King
steps down to servanthood

humbled unto death
emptied willingly

HOW MANY CITIES?

Sometimes I get really frustrated with the Bible. There are places where it makes a statement which triggers a dozen questions in my mind, and then says absolutely nothing to elaborate on it. One of those places is in 1 Chronicles 7:24. The first nine chapters of 1 Chronicles are nothing but lists – so-and-so was the father of such-and-such. Most of the time when I am reading through the Bible I simply skip over them. In the middle of those lists is this totally frustrating statement: "His daughter was Sheerah, who built Beth Horon the lower and the upper, and Uzzen Sheerah." Now I would love for God to have included at least a chapter about this lady in His Word. Who was she? What was she like? What amazing qualities did she have that allowed her to build three cities at a time when it was most definitely a man's world? The Bible doesn't even comment on the unusualness of it, much less tell us how it all came about. She must have been some lady! Nearly four thousand years later, her accomplishment still stands in the Word of God.

Although the Bible tells us nothing about this lady other than her name and her accomplishment, there are several things which we can safely surmise about her.

Firstly, she did not allow herself to be limited by the prevailing mindset. There can't have been very many women in eighteenth century B.C. Israel who woke up one morning and said to themselves, "Now what shall I do today? Shall I weave a mat? Shall I tan some hides? I know, I'll go and build a city!" The culture of the day was very much male-dominated, to the extent that most women didn't even get to share in the family inheritance. Women were for child bearing, house keeping and agricultural labour. Yet that prevailing mindset did not prevent Sheerah from thinking outside the square. Have you allowed others to dictate what you can do, not based on any limitation in Scripture but simply on the prevailing mindset? Have you failed to do something you thought – or even knew – that you were meant to do, simply because nobody else was doing it, or nobody else thought it possible, right or sensible to do it?

Secondly, she had a big vision. Where many would have been content to build a house, she not only built one city, but built three of them. So many people are prepared to settle for a small vision, just as much as they can be comfortable with. It may be that God wants to stretch you, that His vision for your life is far greater than you can presently imagine.

Thirdly, she must have had great people skills, whether natural or developed. Whilst she is credited with building the cities, there had to have been other people, most of them men, who were involved in the actual labour. They carried out what must have been a fairly demanding task under the direction of a woman, in a culture where such a thing was virtually unheard of. Any vision worth accomplishing will take more than we can do by ourselves. If we are to bring it to fulfilment we will need to cultivate those skills which would encourage others to take hold of the vision and work with us toward its fulfilment.

Finally, she knew how to push through and overcome adversity. The fact that she lived in a hostile land and had limited resources did not deter her. No matter what we try to do in God, we are sure to encounter opposition, both from other people and from spiritual forces. We need to learn to keep our vision focused and press on through the difficulties.

Sheerah left a legacy for those of her time, three cities in which they could live and work and carry out commerce. She also left a legacy for us. The cities have long since crumbled to dust, and we have no record of what she was like as a person, nor do we know if she had a family or anything about them. What we do know is that a woman, living in an age that said it couldn't be done, with people many of whom undoubtedly said it shouldn't be done, built three cities.

What if you and I were to break free of the restrictions of the mindset of our time? What if we were to allow God to expand our vision beyond our own comfort zone to something of lasting value? What if we were to allow God to develop in us the skills and character which would encourage people to work with us rather than opposing us? What if we were to determine that, no matter what difficulties were to stand in our way, we would press on toward the goal? Is there maybe a possibility that we also could leave a legacy not only for those who immediately follow us, but for others many years down the track, should the Lord tarry? How many cities will you build?

HOW TO WRECK A PARTY

The people had it all figured out. They needed a king – not the weak, insipid Roman puppet Herod, but a real king who would rally the people and cause them to rise up and throw off the Roman tyranny. They needed someone who would stir up national pride and restore the nation to the greatness it had known in the days of David and Solomon.

They had watched Jesus. They saw in Him a man who had authority like no other they had ever known. When He preached, He did not quote the thoughts and opinions of others as their Rabbis did; He simply declared, "I say unto you..." When the religious authorities, the Pharisees or the Sadducees, tried to trip Him up, as they so often did, He could tie them up in knots seemingly without even trying. Then there was the authority He asserted over nature, commanding wind and waves to be still and loaves and fished to be multiplied; the authority He had over sickness and demons, commanding both with equal ease to leave human bodies; even the authority He demonstrated over death, calling back from its clutches those who had departed this life. If ever there was a man who had the authority to be king, it was Jesus.

They saw that He was popular, at least with everyone other than the religious authorities. Of course, it could be because He healed the sick, did miracles, provided food.... but somehow there was more. People were drawn to Him, from the little children who flocked around Him (much to His disciples displeasure) to those who traveled miles on foot to hear Him preach, to the religious leaders who came secretly to receive what they dare not request publicly. What's more, not only did the people come, but He accepted them. He was not above mixing with tax collectors and fishermen, yet He was not out of place in the company of theologians and rulers. If ever there was a man who had the popularity to be king, it was Jesus.

They saw that He was inspiring. When He spoke, thousands hung on His every word. More than that, lives changed. Prostitutes became evangelists, tax collectors became disciples. Downtrodden people who had believed they were nothing and would always be nothing, began to see themselves with new eyes. Heads that had been permanently bent were held high, eyes that had been dulled with hopelessness shone with the light of life and hope. If ever there was a man with the inspirational power to be king, it was Jesus.

So their course of action was decided. They staged a triumphal procession, a procession which effectively declared Jesus to be king. Waving palm branches and throwing their cloaks on the road in front of the donkey He was riding, they shouted Hosanna! and called Him the king of Israel. No doubt the idea was to follow the pattern of the Old Testament, leading Him to the Temple and there publicly crowning Him as king.

There was just one tiny flaw in the plan. Jesus. Apparently, it had never occurred to the instigators of this thrilling scenario that Jesus may not actually want to be king. That He may reject – or worse, simply ignore – the idea. That He may, in fact, have a quite different agenda. When they planned this party, they had not counted on the honored guest wrecking it!

Jesus saw with very different eyes. He knew that He was the rightful King of Israel, but that the Kingdom he was to rule was vastly different from the one the Jews envisaged. He knew that He was headed for a throne, but He also knew that He would get there by way of a Cross, not a triumphal procession.

Sadly, for many the disappointment of their wrecked party was too much. The next time they surrounded Jesus they would not be waving palms and shouting "Hosanna! Blessed be the King of Israel!", but waving clenched fists and shouting, "Crucify Him! Crucify Him!"

Has God ever wrecked your party? Have you planned that things would go such a way, and seen exactly how God could fit into the picture to make it happen, only to have Him do something totally different and leave you with egg on your face? What is your response? Do you praise God that He knows better than you, or do you turn against Him in anger?

I KNOW THE PLANS I HAVE FOR YOU

God's grace always amazes me, and never more so than when it is extended right in the midst of man's rebellion. God doesn't even wait for our response of repentance before He makes His grace, and its availability, known.

It has been the same right from the beginning, when man first fell into sin. There in the garden the man and the woman stood naked and trembling before Him, having just committed the first human sin, a sin which would rob them of paradise and of their relationship with God, and would plunge the whole of mankind into the mire of sin from which no person, by his own effort, would ever be able to escape. God made His displeasure very clear to them by cursing both them personally and the earth on account of them. But first He turned His attention to the serpent, the real cause of the problem, and in the midst of His curse on the serpent extended the hope and promise of His grace to the man and woman. "I will put hostility between you and the woman, and between your offspring and her offspring. He will bruise your head, and you will bruise his heel." (Genesis 3:15). The curse on man and the earth would not be forever. One would come who would destroy the destroyer, even though it would cost Him dearly to do so, and through Him God's grace would be extended to all mankind.

Thousands of years later, God was again pronouncing judgement against His people. Jeremiah was just one of a long string of prophets who had confronted the people of God with their sins, and called them to turn back to the worship of the true God and the practices of righteousness, justice and mercy. Sometimes they had responded for a little while, only to quickly fall back into their old ways when the prophet left the scene. Now God had had enough. It was past the time for chances. It was even past the time for intercession, for several times in the book of Jeremiah God tells His servant not to pray for the people. God's mind was made up; His judgement was set in stone. Nothing was going to stop the people from being taken to exile in Babylon. And, once they were there, nothing was going to shorten the time of their banishment. "Build houses and settle down," God tells them. "Plant gardens and eat what they produce." (Jeremiah 29:5) They were going to be in exile for a long time; they might as well get used to it.

Yet here again, right in the midst of God's judgement, is the offer and promise of God's grace: "I know the plans I have for you..... plans to prosper you and not to harm you, plans to give you a hope and a future." (Jeremiah 29:11) They had chosen to worship the false gods of the nations around them, and God had handed them over to their choices, but it was not God's desire for them. It was not His best. They were still in rebellion, yet even before they repented and turned back to Him God was extending to them the offer of an even deeper relationship with Himself.

God deals even more graciously with us. His provision of salvation, forgiveness, healing, justification, adoption, sanctification, and everything we could ever need was made through the death of Jesus long before any of us were even born. It was extended to us whilst we were still lost in sin. In fact, God not only offered us His great salvation package, He actively pursued us with it. Like the Hound of Heaven, the Holy Spirit sought us till we found Him.

More than that, even when we move away from God, He comes after us. His desire is not to punish and harm us, but to draw us lovingly into a deeper relationship with Himself. It is only when we blatantly refuse His advances that He will move to more drastic means to get our attention. Even then, His purpose is not to destroy us, but to turn us back. The very punishment is itself an act of grace extended to us.

How much better it is if we don't force His hand to that point! Take hold of His offer of grace, His offer of a future and a hope. Seek Him with all your heart, and His promise is that He will be found.

IN THE NAME OF JESUS

"In Jesus' Name." How regularly we tag those words on to the end of a prayer. Often we do it without even really thinking about what we are saying: it is just a formula, an extension of the "amen" which for most of us is simply a meaningless word, another way of saying "I've finished praying now."

"In the name of Her Majesty, Queen Elizabeth of England." Would we use those words as easily? The idea seems almost laughable! Proclamations in the name of the Queen can only be made by those who have been given authority by her. Even then, the thing they are proclaiming has to be something that the Queen has actually decreed. No-one would even think of declaring in the Queen's name something that was purely out of their own wishes and desires - and if they did think of it, and carried that thought into action, they could expect to face at best a lengthy jail term. On the other hand, when someone who has been authorised by the Queen makes in her name a proclamation that she has decreed, then that proclamation has authority to see that thing carried out, or to enforce penalties if it is not.

This applies even at a more mundane level. If mother tells Johnny, "Go tell Bobby I said to come in from play now," then when Johnny goes to deliver the message it is the same as if Mother were speaking to Bobby personally. There is no use Bobby saying, "But it was only Johnny who told me!" Johnny went in Mother's name, and therefore with her authority. However, if Johnny takes it upon himself to tell Bobby, "Mother said you are to give my your baseball bat," it's a totally different story. Mother said no such thing, and Johnny had no right to attach her name to his wishes. Not only does his demand not carry Mother's authority, it is also likely to earn Johnny some strong discipline.

Jesus told His disciples, and through them, us: "Whatsoever you ask the Father in My Name, He will give it to you." Many of us have taken that as meaning that we can ask for anything we please, and as long as we tack "in Jesus' Name" on the end, those words will be the magic wand that make God give us what we want.

We've got it back to front! The person issuing a decree in the name of Queen Elizabeth must first go into her presence and hear what it is she wants, and how it is to be said. If the decree is to carry the Queen's authority, then it must be exactly what she wants. Johnny must carry to Bobby his mother's wishes, not his own.

If this is true of any human situation where we speak in the name and authority of another, why can we not see that it is also true when we dare to speak in the greatest Name and the highest authority, that of the Lord Jesus Christ? His Name is not a magic wand to materialise our wishes. His Name is His authority, and His authority is based on His will.

Before we tack His Name on to the end of our prayers, we need to come into His presence. We need to bring our situations, our needs, our desires to Him, and hear from His throne what He wants to do about them. Then, confident that we are declaring the will of the Lord, we can add "in Jesus' Name" to our prayers and decrees, knowing that indeed they are backed by all the authority of heaven.

If we don't, we risk not only not having the authority of heaven, but actually being in defiance of God. Remember the commandment that says, "Do not take the Name of the Lord in vain"? We have taken this to refer to blasphemy, but surely using the Name of Jesus to back decrees that are not His but ours qualifies as using His Name "in vain."

Of course, there are those who go to the opposite extreme. Rather than bring their own desires and declare them to be authorized by Jesus, they pray "if it be Thy will" prayers - and still tag "in Jesus' Name" on the end of them! "If it be Thy will" prayers are meaningless. They are basically a way of washing our hands of the situation and saying, "God, do whatever You want." They are an abdication of our responsibility to find God's will in the situation and pray accordingly.

Some people base this kind of praying on Jesus' prayer in the Garden of Gethsemane, "Not My will but Yours." Jesus, however, was not saying, "I can't be bothered finding Your will so just do whatever You please." He knew the will of the Father: it was that Jesus go to the Cross. Rather than avoiding that will, Jesus embraced it. He said in effect, "Everything in My human will wants to avoid this, but I know that this is Your will, Father, so I submit My human will to Your will. I choose what You want, not what I want."

Jesus wants us to pray in His Name. He has given us authority to pray in His Name. But our authority is always a derived authority. To speak effectively in His Name, we have to be speaking the things that He wants. We have to take the time to hear His heart and will in the matter. When we do, we will find ourselves speaking with an authority that heaven will not resist - and that hell can not resist.

WAR IN HEAVEN

The ancient battle lines have now been drawn.
No more this occupation will be borne.
The saints' accuser vile
Permitted for a while
Now from Jehovah's presence shall be thrown.

Michael, Prince of angels, stands to fight.
The enemy responds with all his might.
But victory has been planned
Since ever time began
For darkness has no power over light.

The Blood that seals this battle has been shed
Not by this army's body, but its Head
God's spotless lamb was given
His flesh by man's sin riven
Man's life by His redeemed now from the dead.

Through years the store of potent swords has grown -
The words and lives of those who are His own
Bought back from death's dark hold
In witness fiercely bold
With Him their lives in battle gladly sown.

Now at last the triumph has been sealed.
Impotent, the enemy must yield.
Hurled down from his place
Now against the race
of man, enraged, his fury he will wield.

Open fully now the heavens stand
No longer now is God shut off from man.
Those who would grasp God's power

Are free in this last hour
To rise in His authority and take the land.

IT IS FINISHED!

In some ways it was the darkest day of human history, a day which above all others would be written in infamy. It was the day on which man's degradation and rebellion hit its lowest point: the day on which created beings rose up to seek to destroy their creator. It was the day on which evil killed righteousness, on which guilt killed innocence. It would have been a day of unrelenting darkness, except for two things.

The first thing that changed this day from the darkest of human history to the greatest was the fact that, even though it was man that carried out the actions, the plan was from start to end God's. In fact, He had known this day would come even before He created the very beings who would make it necessary. Man's sin never took God by surprise. He knew it was coming, and He knew what He planned to do about it. Before ever He created man, before ever He gave man free will, He knew the terrible price He would pay to bring man back to Himself. Jesus Christ was the "Lamb slain from the foundation of the world."

Yes, Calvary was the expression of the depth of human sin; but more than that, it was the expression of the far greater depths of God's love. Though men and devils saw it as the defeat of the Son of God, it was in fact the greatest victory this world has ever seen.

That is because at Calvary Jesus reversed Adam's sin. Where Adam disobeyed, Jesus obeyed. Where Adam sought to raise himself up in pride, Jesus brought Himself down in humility. Where Adam gratified the flesh, Jesus allowed His flesh to be destroyed.

It is important that we understand that Calvary was not just the payment of the debt of individual sin, as wonderful as that in itself is. Far more than that, Jesus not only paid for but reversed the sin of mankind. Where Adam had led mankind off to follow after satan, Jesus gave His life to lead men back to God. Adam handed dominion to the devil, Jesus won the Kingdom back.

Calvary was not a job half done. Jesus did not pay for just some of the sin of mankind, or for just some of the sin of any one individual. He paid the price in full. He did not win half a victory, but total victory. Colossians speaks firstly of Him "wiping out the handwriting in ordinances which was against us. He has taken it out of the way, nailing it to the cross." This speaks of the writing of God's just judgement which was against each one of us. In Roman times a prisoner's charge and sentence would be written on a scroll which was hung outside his cell so that everyone could see what this person had done, and the penalty he was paying. Jesus took each of our "scrolls" and nailed them to the cross, declaring Himself to be the prisoner paying that penalty in our place. When the sentence was completed, the authority would write across the scroll, "It is finished", which meant "paid in full". The scroll was then given to the prisoner to prove that he was justly free, and had no more of his sentence to serve. When Jesus was about to die, He cried out those same words, "It is finished!", not as a cry of defeat, but as a shout of victory proclaiming that He had indeed paid the full price for freedom for each and every person. For each of us, this means that when we come to Jesus He declares us "not guilty." We do not have to atone for our sins. If we had to, we could never have done it. But Jesus has done it for us. We simply need to walk in the righteousness He has given us.

Colossians then speaks of Jesus "Having stripped the principalities and the powers, he made a show of them openly, triumphing over them in it." Here the language is that of a Roman triumphal procession. The victorious general would ride into the city on his stallion, with those he had conquered walking – or being dragged – behind, stripped and chained to his chariot wheels, totally defeated and helpless. The Word of God says that is what Jesus did to principalities and powers, and He did it not by a display of His almighty strength, but by weakness and apparent defeat. For us, it means that we don't have to fight demonic powers, whether it be some petty little nuisance-value-only demon right up to Satan himself. They are already defeated. We simply need to learn to stand in the victory that Jesus has already won.

Yet all that would be just a nice theory without the second thing which turns that first Good Friday from a day of darkness to a day of triumph. That thing is Sunday morning – that great, glorious moment when Life proved that it could never be confined in death, when mortality reclaimed immortality, when the Father declared His acceptance and approval of the Son and crowned Jesus' "It is finished!" with "It is accepted, it is sealed, and it stands forever!"

Have you really accepted that "It is finished" for you personally? That your sin has been dealt with once and for all, and the righteousness of God made freely available to you in Christ? That every demon you will ever face has already been defeated and made a public spectacle by Christ? That the battle has already been won, and you (if you are in Christ) are on the winning side? If you are still struggling, ask God to make this a reality for you today. Let this Easter establish in your life, once for all, all that that first Easter made available for you.

OF LAME DUCKS AND EAGLES

The husband of a friend of mine refers to her as a "collector of lame ducks". By this he means, of course, not the feathered kind, but people with problems. These are the kind of people who are highly dependent, unable to get by in life without someone else to prop them up.

All of us have problems from time to time, and in those periods it is important for us to know that there is someone who cares, someone who will stand beside us and help us to carry the burden. In fact Scripture exhorts us to do this for other people.

There are also those who have permanent mental disabilities, just as there are those with permanent physical disabilities. Unless these people receive a healing from the Lord, they will always be dependent. They need our compassion and support, and most of all our prayers.

However, there are also lame ducks who don't really need to be lame. They could be better, if only they would learn to let go of the things that bind them and rise up in the power of the Lord. Some of them have never learned that this is possible, and so are held captive by ignorance. Others have been taught over and over again, but somehow, whether consciously or unconsciously, the comfort they receive from being dependent is greater to them than the possibility of freedom. They are emotional hypochondriacs, clinging to every problem, and constantly looking for new ones. They are the people who are on every prayerline, who know every counsellor in town, and who drive the pastor to distraction with constant phone calls. They need someone else to pray on their behalf, to make their decisions for them, and to hold their hands through every step of life. If someone challenges them to grow up in God, they will cry, "I can't. Can't you see I'm lame. How could you be so cruel as to expect a lame duck to walk unaided?"

Then there are the eagles. I live in a house perched high on a hill, and I am blessed to have a pair of eagles who often soar around the property. I think their nest must be somewhere nearby. What a joy it is to watch these magnificent, graceful birds gliding on the air currents. By contrast, I recently watched a smaller bird trying to fly against a strong headwind. It was flapping its wings with all its might, but still going backwards rather than forwards. Eagles, on the other hand, hardly flap at all. They simply find the air current they want and allow it to do the work.

What a lessen the eagle is for us as Christians. God has provided the wind of the Holy Spirit to carry us where He wants us to go. The Spirit can help us to soar above our problems and enable us to have a God's-eye-view of them. When we see things from God's perspective, the problems which seemed huge to us when we stood face to face with them dwindle to insignificance.

There is another lesson to be learned from the eagle. It doesn't try to kill its prey itself. Instead, it carries the prey to great heights, then drops it on rocks. If that doesn't work the first time, it does it again and again until the animal is dead. No fighting or wrestling, simply lift and drop.

We can learn to do that with our problems: simply lift them before the throne of our mighty God, *and then drop them*. All too often we lift our problems before the throne, hold them there for a brief moment, then carry them off to try to wrestle them into submission ourselves. We have to learn, like the eagle, to simply lift and drop, and if necessary to keep lifting and dropping until the problem is well and truly dead.

Are you a lame duck or an eagle? If you are a lame duck, know that you can change. By the power and grace of God you can not only become a completely healthy duck, you can become an eagle. To do it, you will have to make some changes. The first of those is to be prepared for change. Many lame ducks stay as they are because they are afraid to get better. They are afraid that they will lose their friends if they no longer need support, and that they will be left alone. However, friendship between equally free people is much more enjoyable than friendship in which one is constantly unhealthily dependent upon the other. You have everything to gain by growth, and nothing to lose but your pain.

Secondly, begin to do some small things for yourself. Make some small decisions. Even if they turn out to be wrong, it is better than not having decided at all. Most of all, begin to pray for yourself. You don't have to pray great, long, fancy prayers. Simply "Father, please help me with this area of my life" is a good beginning. You can still ask your friends to stand with you in agreement; that is quite different from asking them to pray in your place.

Most of all, take hold of God's word that says, "Those who wait upon the Lord shall renew their strength, they shall rise up on wings as eagles". That word is for all of us, including lame ducks!

If you are a collector of lame ducks, maybe you would like to share this message with them.

PRAY IMPOSSIBLE PRAYERS

Recently I have become totally frustrated with some of my own praying, and much of the praying I hear from others in the Body of Christ. We have settled for praying for the possible, the easy, the comfortable. "Let the operation be successful." "Help him find a suitable job." "Provide a home for them." All good prayers, but easily within the realm of possibility.

I can no longer be content praying for the possible. My God is infinite. Omnipotent. Omniscient. And very much still on the throne. I want to engage fully with Him. I want – need – to pray impossible prayers. I want to call on Him for the miracles I know He wants to give. There are too many impossible situations – situations that only God can change - in our world today to spend all our prayer on the possible.

One of the areas of impossible prayer that has been a passion of mine for some years, is praying for terrorists. When a terrorist is named in the media, he becomes a target for prayer. As I see it, if you kill a terrorist, a dozen others will quickly rise to take his place; but if he has an encounter with God and is transformed into a follower of Christ, he will probably drag a dozen or more into the Kingdom with him. Saul of Tarsus was the terrorist of his day, and just look what God did with him.

Just recently I have realised that this does not have to be applied only to terrorists. Those who promote godless agenda, those who bring in legislation to limit the effectiveness of the church, those who promote the destruction of human life whether at its beginning or at its end – all of them could be turned away from their current path by an encounter with the living God. All of them are legitimate targets for "impossible" prayer.

Aside from the effect of individuals being brought out of the kingdom of darkness and into the Kingdom of God, imagine the effect in the spiritual realm if, every time

LAW AND GRACE

One of the greatest problems that faced the early Church was that of the Judaisers - those people who wanted to force the Gentiles to accept Jewish laws and traditions before they could become Christians. Sadly, two thousand years later, they are still around and still creating problems. They range from the "Sabbath keepers" who insist that the only legitimate day to worship is Saturday to the "Torah observers" who insist that Christians are still bound by the laws of the Old Covenant to the "Hebrew speakers" who insist that anyone who uses an English (or presumably any other language) translation of God's Name is committing blasphemy. Some even insist, despite all the evidence to the contrary, that the New Testament was written in Hebrew. I'm sure there are other varieties around as well.

They all sound very learned and holy, and it would be easy for an immature Christian, or one who does not know the Word very well, to be carried away with their teachings. Therefore it is very important for Christians to understand the relationship between Law and Grace.

What do we mean by the Law? Many people think that "the Law" refers only to the Ten Commandments, but it is much, much broader than that. Biblically speaking, the first five books of the Bible - Genesis, Exodus, Leviticus, Numbers and Deuteronomy - are referred to collectively as "the Law." Bible scholars tell us that those books contain 613 commandments (although I have read those books many times, I have never counted the commandments - I am happy to take the scholars' word.) In fact, when Jesus was asked, "What is the greatest commandment IN THE LAW?" He did not quote from the Ten Commandments, but from Deuteronomy 6:5 ("You shall love the Lord your God with all your heart, with all your soul, and with all your mind") and Leviticus 19:18 ("You shall love your neighbour as yourself.") (Matt22:36-39)

The first thing we need to understand about the Law is that it was never given to the Gentiles. It was part of God's covenant with the nation of Israel. It was not the means by which Israel entered into covenant with God - they were in covenant with Him because they were descendants of Abraham. In that sense the Old Covenant, like the New, was a covenant of grace. No Israelite could say that he was an Israelite because of his own goodness or effort or scholarship or anything else he had done: he was an Israelite only because God had caused him to be born into the family of Israel, and because he was an Israelite he was in covenant relationship with the God of Abraham. The Law told him how he was to live in that covenant relationship. Never in the entire Old Testament is a Gentile individual or nation rebuked by God for not keeping the terms of His covenant with Israel, except when they interfered with Israel's keeping of the covenant.

We should not imagine that the Law was arbitrary, like the rules of a game that might be changed at whim. Rather, every aspect of the Law reflected the character of God. The moral laws reflected His righteousness; the criminal laws reflected His justice; the social laws reflected His mercy; the laws of purity and separation reflected His holiness; the sacrificial laws reflected His redemptive purposes.

As a reflection of God's character, the Law was good. There was just one problem: the Law could set a standard for man, but it could not give man the ability to live up to that standard. Between the Fall and the Day of Pentecost, people did not have the Holy Spirit living within them. He came upon some people - notably prophets, but also a few others - to enable to carry out the work to which they were called, but He did not live within them. Without that internal compass of the Spirit's presence, people needed something external to show them how to live. The Law fulfilled that purpose wonderfully. But an external standard can never change our hearts: that can only come from within. Therefore what the Law really did, for those who had eyes to see, was to expose their sinfulness and show them just how incapable they were of meeting God's standards, and how much they needed someone to rescue them from their sin. That's why Paul refers to the Law as a "tutor to bring us to Christ" (Galatians 3:24) - but note that in the very next verse he says that when faith has come, we are no longer under the tutor.

He says this even more strongly in Romans 10:4: "For Christ is the fulfillment of the law for righteousness to everyone who believes." Again in Galatians 5:18: "But if you are led by the Spirit you are not under the Law."

Does that mean that we can now do as we please - murder, steal, commit adultery, or anything else we like because we are no longer under the Law? As Paul would say, "God forbid!" It is not that we are not subject to any law, but rather that we are subject to a different law: the law of the Spirit of life in Christ Jesus. (Romans 8:2)

Unlike the people of the Old Covenant, as New Covenant believers in the Lord Jesus Christ we have the Spirit of God living within our renewed human spirits. The Law reflected God's nature; the Spirit bears God's nature. The Law showed us how to live; the Spirit enables us to live. It is not that we have a lower standard - in fact, the standard of the Spirit is higher than that of the Law could ever be.

Jesus began to point to this in His "You have heard it said ... but I say unto you..." statements in Matthew 5:22ff. In each case, He pointed His followers to a standard that was far higher than that required by the Law. Why? If they couldn't keep the lower standard of the Law, how did He ever expect them to keep these higher standards? The answer, of course, is that He didn't. He was trying to cut through the self righteousness that imagined it could live up to God's standards in its own ability. He was trying to show them that to live God's kind of life, they needed to have God's life.

Some will object that the Spirit only enables us to live according to the Law, having the Spirit does not exempt us from the Law. However, Paul's schoolmaster illustration makes it clear that this is not the case. We do not stay in school forever. Once we have learned the lessons that we need, we move on. The laws that ruled us when we were in school no longer apply. Even when the laws of the adult world are the same as the laws at school - for instance, stealing is not allowed at school, nor is it allowed in the adult world - once we leave school we are not obeying the school's law not to steal, but the adult world's law not to steal.

Let's use another illustration: I was born in Australia and have lived in this country all my life, but let's pretend I go to live in India. Both India and Australia have a law that says you cannot commit murder. If I were to commit murder whilst I am here in Australia, I would of course be tried under Australian law, which I would have broken. However, if I move to India, I am no longer under Australian law, but under Indian law. If I then commit murder, it is Indian law I have broken, and Indian law under which I will be tried. On the other hand, I have never lived in Brazil. I am sure Brazil also has laws against murder, but I cannot break the Brazilian law against murder no matter how many people I kill in either Australia or India, because I have never been subject to Brazilian law.

Remember, the Law of the Old Testament was part of God's covenant with Israel. It was never given to the Gentiles. When the Gentiles began to come into the Church and the council was held to decide what should be done with them, the apostles did not tell them to keep the Law, or to observe the Sabbath, or to be circumcised. Rather, they gave them three simple principles: abstain from strangled animals, from blood, and from sexual immorality. Neither was this a matter of man throwing out God's Law, for they said "It seemed good to the Holy Spirit and to us ..." (Acts 15:28) This was a matter of much prayer, and the result was directed by the Spirit. Not only was the Law never given to the Gentiles in the Old Testament, it was also never given to the Gentiles in the New. If you are a Gentile, you have never lived in "Law Land!" The laws of Law Land do not apply to you. That does not mean that you did not sin. Sin is more than breaking the commandments - sin is falling short of the glory of God. (Romans 3:23) If you have repented your sin and accepted the Lord Jesus Christ as your Saviour, and are trusting in His grace and nothing else, you live in "Spirit Land" and are under the law of the Spirit.

If you are a Jew who has become a Christian, then you have moved from Law Land to Spirit Land. You are no longer under the laws of Law Land, but under the law of the Spirit.

The law of the Spirit is not like the Law of the Old Testament, which set up an external standard but did not give people the ability to meet that standard. The law of the Spirit works by transformation, not by regulation. As we surrender to the rule of the Holy Spirit in our lives, he transforms us into the likeness of Christ "from one degree of glory to another." (2 Corinthians 3:18) Now we do not kill, not because the Law forbids it, but because the God into whose likeness we are being transformed is a life giver; we do not commit adultery, not because of the Law, but because we are being changed to be like our holy God.

So, what about Jesus' statement that "not one jot or tittle" would pass from the Law (Matthew 5:18; Luke 16:17)? Firstly, Jesus fulfilled the Law, not only in its letter but in its spirit. He is the only person who has ever lived who has done so. In fact, it was only His perfect fulfilment of the Law that qualified Him to be the Saviour of mankind. His divinity did not qualify Him: to be the Saviour He had to be human, and He had to have no sin of His own against Him. In Him the Law was perfectly fulfilled for all who will come to Him.

However, the Law has not passed away. It is still there, and its penalties are still there, for those who choose to live under it. Paul says, "For as many as have sinned without law shall also perish without law: and as many as have sinned in the law shall be judged by the law;" (Romans 2:12) In other words, those who choose to come under the Law of the Old Testament must fulfil all of it - all 613 laws found in the Pentateuch - for to break any part of it is sin. At the same time, those who were never under the Law are still without excuse: God created us in His likeness, and every time we fall short of that likeness it is sin.

Whether for a Jew who was subject to the Law of the Old Testament, or for a Gentile who was never subject to it, the wages of sin is death. (Roman 6:13) Our choice is simple: receive those wages ourselves, or receive Christ who reaped them on our behalf.

If we accept Christ, He freely extends His righteousness to us. That's grace. That's life. That's Spirit Land.

If we choose to live under the Law, we must provide our own righteousness. That's bondage. That's death. That's Law Land.

We can choose to live in Law Land, or in Spirit Land, but there is no dual citizenship: we cannot do both at the same time.

LIVING IN THE ANOINTING

"As for you, the anointing which you received from him remains in you, and you don't need for anyone to teach you. But as his anointing teaches you concerning all things, and is true, and is no lie, and even as it taught you, you will remain in him. " 1 John 2:27

I had been in a desert for a long time. Prayer, which once had flowed so freely, had become an impossible task. Every gift in which I had once moved seemed to have become dead on the vine. God seemed to have gone off to attend to other things, leaving me to my own devices. With Him, He had taken all my joy, my hope, my faith. I was within a breath of simply walking away from everything.

Then I saw something that alerted me to the activity of the enemy of souls in a particular area. With enough faith to make a grain of mustard seed look like a mountain, I began to pray, and then to move from speaking to the Lord to addressing the enemy. And suddenly it was there. Suddenly what came out of my mouth was not just words, dispersing into the atmosphere the moment they left my lips. Suddenly there was the old familiar feeling of the oil of the Spirit pouring over my spirit, the familiar sharp edge as my words became a sword, the familiar sense of standing toe to toe with the enemy, staring him down, and watching him back off.

The situation I was addressing was one that was far bigger than my personal life. I had no objective way of assessing the impact of my words. Yet I know they were effective, because my personal spiritual atmosphere changed dramatically in that instant.

Suddenly, I had moved into the anointing.

Had I lost it during that long time in the desert? Had the anointing gone off somewhere, only to return at the opportune moment? No, this verse in 1 John makes it clear that the anointing remains. I had lost touch with it, but it was still there.

So what is the anointing anyway? It is the power with which the Holy Spirit infuses our natural or spiritual gifts, so that they flow not out of us, but out of Him. More than that, it is the power by which He infuses our lives so that His ability and authority flow through us.

Each one of us has a spiritual destiny in God. The anointing is the equipment God gives us to enable us to fulfil that spiritual destiny.

The anointing is inextricably linked with the Holy Spirit. When we are born again, the Holy Spirit comes to live within us. With Him, He brings the anointing.

That, however, does not mean that we will automatically walk in the anointing, or that, having once walked in it, we will continue to do so. It takes a shift on our part: a shift out of the realm of the soul and into the realm of the spirit. A shift out of the seen and into the unseen.

First, we must believe that we have the anointing. Even if we have lost the *feeling* of it, we must know in our heart that God has given us His Spirit to equip us for everything that He will ever ask of us. Sometimes that may mean hanging on by our fingernails, believing despite every evidence of our eyes.

Then we must step into it, regardless of how we feel. That may mean quoting the truth of God's Word even if it feels like an empty ritual. That morning as I said, "Lord, I take up the authority You have given me..." I did not feel any anointing. I did not feel any authority. I said it purely because I know it is true: Jesus said, "I give you authority over all the power of the enemy." Some would say God responded to my faith, but I gotta tell you, I didn't have any! God responded to His Word.

His Word says that we each have an anointing: we have His supernatural empowerment for whatever He has called us to do. When we take hold of that anointing, He honours His Word and releases His power into our lives.

MORE THAN A BLIND EYE

As I have observed the Church over the years, it seems to me that most Christians have at best a very poor grasp of the concept of grace.

There are those who ignore grace altogether, believing that the only way they are ever going to make it to heaven is if they somehow manage to stay on the straight-and-narrow, and along the way do enough good works to earn them plenty of brownie points. Of course, in a Biblical sense, such people are not really Christians at all. They follow a philosophy or a religion, but they have never really embraced and surrendered to the Person, the Lord Jesus Christ. The Bible makes it very clear that all our "goodness" and "good works" will add up to nothing when we stand before God, if we do not stand cleansed and forgiven through the shed blood of Jesus. Salvation is by grace, it is a gift. We cannot earn grace, we do not deserve it, and nothing we can ever do will stand in place of it.

Others see grace as merely God turning a blind eye to our sin, like a kind of benevolent grandfather who simply pats us on the head and smiles benignly when we do wrong. They think that the fact that they can never deserve grace by "being good" excuses them from being good, and that they can never earn it by good works exempts them from good works. No matter what they do, they reason, God's grace will still be extended to them.

This is as wrong a concept of grace as those have who ignore it. It is promoted by the standard Evangelical definition of grace as "God's unmerited favor." Whilst certainly not untrue, that definition is like defining a Lambourgini as "a car." It doesn't even come close to telling it all.

The first use of the word "grace" (Greek "charis") in the New Testament is in Luke 2:40, where it says that the grace of God was on the boy Jesus. Now Jesus never sinned, so He did not need the Father to turn a blind eye to anything that He had done. Since He was equal with the Father in every way, it also could not be said that He did not merit the Father's favour. In fact, at His baptism 18 years later the Father publicly declared that He was well pleased with Him.

The grace that was on Jesus, then, was something quite different. From the context, it is obviously referring to something of God's character: Jesus was, in every way, a true representation of the Father. Since exactly the same word is used for grace when it refers to us, it must have for us the same connotation: grace imparts to us something of the character of God. Unlike Jesus, of course, we are not deserving of that impartation. In a different way, it is God's unmerited favour to us.

Grace – still the same word – is seen in another aspect in Acts 4:33. After the release of Peter and John from prison, the church prayed powerfully for their ongoing work and witness, and the Scripture declares, "With great power the apostles continued to testify to the resurrection of the Lord Jesus, and much grace was upon them all." Again, it is not talking about the grace of seeing their sins forgiven, but of power and influence in their ministry.

Paul, in Romans 1:5, speaks of himself as receiving "grace (still the same word) and apostleship to call people from among all the Gentiles to the obedience that comes from faith." Paul was not speaking of his salvation, but of his ministry. He recognised that his call to the office of apostle was not because of his goodness or anything he had done, but by God's unmerited favor. More than that, he understood that he could never fulfill the requirements of that office in his own strength, but was totally dependent upon the power and anointing of God's Spirit.

It would take a whole book – perhaps several – to fully look into the various aspects of grace. Since we don't have that kind of time or space available right now, I would simply like to suggest a new definition for your consideration: "God's mighty power working in you to achieve that which you do not deserve and which you could not achieve by yourself." In other words, grace is God's ability: God's ability to take hold by faith on the merits of Jesus' death on your behalf. God's ability to live in a way that is pleasing to Him. God's ability to fulfill whatever works He has called you to do. God's ability to forgive others as He has forgiven you. God's ability to stand strong in whatever temptations, difficulties or persecutions come against you. God's ability, every breath, every heart beat, every moment.

When we understand grace this way, we see why it can never be just a "blind eye" to sin. Grace is a package deal. We cannot accept grace to take hold of salvation, without also accepting grace to live a godly life. We cannot accept grace for our own forgiveness without accepting grace for the forgiveness of those who offend us. If we reject one part of the package, we automatically reject the whole package.

Through the death of Jesus, God has made His grace freely available to every one of us. The only question that remains is, will we accept it?

NEW BEGINNINGS

I love New Year. The page of the old year may be frayed around the edges, torn and blotted, with mistakes crossed out and attempts at re-writing, but the New Year presents a brand new page. Not a single stroke has yet been made upon it. What will have been written there by this time next year? Will it be a romance, a comedy or a tragedy? Will it be a song of victory or a dirge of lament? Each year we dare to hope that, this time, we will avoid the mistakes and the blots, and that we will survive the year at least reasonably intact. We bring out all our hopes for change and achievement and dust them off. Perhaps this will be the year we finally have the discipline to keep those resolutions!

One way or another, the New Year is a time of reflection – a time to stop, take a deep breath, and look at our lives. Are we going in the right direction, or are we wandering in ever-decreasing circles? Have we achieved our goals, or have we forgotten that we even had goals in the first place? Are we so "up to our neck in alligators" that we have forgotten that the original plan was to drain the swamp?

Of course, it doesn't have to be limited to New Year. I tend to do the same sort of thing on my birthday and other important anniversaries. The promise of a new beginning is very attractive!

Do you know that God is in the "new beginnings" business? Jesus came, lived and died so that we would be able to have a new beginning with God, no longer carrying the burden of our guilt and sin but set free to be His child. Unlike New Year resolutions, which are a wonderful idea but totally lack the power to carry them through, the new beginning God offers actually comes with an in-built power pack – His is called the Holy Spirit. The Bible tells us, "For it is God who works in you both to will and to work, for his good pleasure." (Phil 2:13) That means the Holy Spirit is able not only to cause us to *want* to do God's will, but to make us able to actually *do it!*

For many, however, the new beginning that came when they surrendered their lives to Jesus is a long time ago. Like last year's New Year resolutions, it has been battered and blotted by the passage of time and life. They wish they could go back and get born again, again. They wish they could know again the joy of their salvation.

If this is you, then there is good news: God offers not just a new beginning, but endless new beginnings. He has given us a priceless gift called repentance. Repentance is not something heavy and horrible, thundered by hairy prophets in animal skins. Repentance is simply running back into Daddy's arms when you have been away. Jesus told the parable of the prodigal son to show that, no matter how far you go away, the Father is waiting, arms outstretched, ready to welcome you back. (Many people think this parable is talking about sinners coming to initial repentance. It is not. The prodigal was already the Father's son before he left, he remained the Father's son while he was away, and he was re-instated as the Father's son when he returned.) Do you need a new beginning? Leave the pig sty behind, run back to Daddy's arms. Run back to relationship. Run back to communion. Run home.

New Year is a great time for reflection and stocktaking. But don't let it wait till New Year. Every new day is a brand new page. No one has ever written on it. No one has yet torn it or blotted it. No one has made mistakes and tried to scratch them out. Better yet, God already knows everything that will be written on it before the day is out.

Why not make every day a new beginning. Take a little time each night to review the day that has been. Repent of the areas where you have "fallen short of God's glory". If you have wandered away during the day, be sure you are home and snuggled tightly up to Him. Take a moment to thank Him for all the blessings and the challenges (which are really a different kind of blessing) that the day has brought. Pause to congratulate yourself on the things you have achieved, reflect on the areas that you failed and resolve to succeed in them tomorrow. Then tie the whole day up in a bundle, hand it to God and say, "Lord, this day is now past. I cannot re-live one moment of it. I cannot undo anything that I have done, or anything that has been done to me, this day. I give it into Your safe keeping. Tomorrow is a new day!" Then sleep well, and wake up to a new beginning.

That's my New Year resolution.

PREGNANT WITH A PROMISE

She was only a young girl, probably still in her early teens, and engaged to be married. Life was pretty good. She was part of a loving family who were faithful in their observance of the Jewish religion, and her fiance was a good, kind man. The future looked comfortable, if not exciting.

Then one day the totally unexpected happened. An unearthly visitor told her that she was chosen to be the mother of Messiah, but that this would mean her becoming pregnant without having relations with a man, by the sovereign overshadowing of the Holy Spirit. The promise was wonderful, totally mind-blowing, but the consequences of the pregnancy could be truly horrible. She would be taken as being a loose woman, for surely no-one would believe her story of a miraculous conception. Her fiance would most likely divorce her (in those days engagement was as binding as marriage, and could only be broken by divorce). Her family would probably disown her. The entire village could be expected to treat her as an outcast. The promise was wonderful, but oh! how costly!

Yet she did not count the cost as too high. "Let it be unto me according to your word." A response of amazingly mature faith from one so young. She was prepared to take hold of God's promise and cling to it, no matter what the cost to see it through.

There are two great differences between the promises of God and the plans of man. The plans of man come from our own thoughts, and can only ever be as big as our thoughts will allow. The promises of God, however, always come by a divine overshadowing. They are created and planted in our spirit by the Holy Spirit, just as the seed of life that was to become Jesus was planted in the womb of Mary. Because they come from an infinite God, they are always far bigger than anything we could ever have planned or dreamed out of our own thoughts. It has been truly said that if your dream isn't big enough to scare you, then it is probably not of God.

Not only are God's promises bigger than our plans, they are also more costly. When we make our plans we protect ourselves, consciously or unconsciously weighing up just how much we are prepared to give to see this thing come about, and carefully ensuring that we do not plan for anything which would cost more than we are prepared to offer. God, however, sets the cost not according to our limited resources and willingness, but according to the value of the promise. Then, if we are prepared to embrace both the promise and the cost, He gives us His resources to meet that cost. First, we have to be willing.

Are you pregnant with a promise of God? Has the Holy Spirit planted in your spirit something which is far bigger than anything you could have thought up, anything you could have dreamed or hoped for? If you are, then you will understand that to carry the promise, and eventually to bring it to birth, involves a cost. Be like Mary, accepting that cost and not allowing it to cause you to reject the promise.

Any woman who has had children will tell you that pregnancy is a time which is both wonderful and horrible. The excitement and hope of the new life growing within is wonderful. The thought of what this child could be, and of the privilege that will be yours in helping to shape and direct this life, is wonderful. The morning sickness, the heartburn, the backache, the tiredness, the feeling of being a blimp, the discomfort, are horrible. Not to mention the pain of labour! However there are very few women who would not say that the horrible aspects of pregnancy are outweighed by the wonderful ones.

If you are pregnant with a promise of God, there will be difficulties between the conception of that promise and its bringing to full birth. There will be times of discomfort. More than that, the promise which is growing within you, like the One who was growing in Mary, has the potential to bring you rejection, scorn, ridicule and condemnation. Just remember that the God who was big enough to give you the promise is also big enough to bring it to fulfilment. You do not have the resources to meet the challenges that your promise will bring, but He does. Just as a pregnant woman to a large degree focuses inward, thinking about the life that is growing within her, so focus on the promise, hold it before God in faith, lean on Him and trust in Him.

As surely as there dawned the day which we celebrate as Christmas, your promise will also come to birth in the time of God's appointment. Yet even that is not the end of it. For Mary, both the promise and the pain continued throughout her life. They were present in her Son's childhood, ministry, death, resurrection, and ascension. So it is for every parent. And so it is for all those who are pregnant with the promises of God. You cannot bring the promise to birth and then leave it as a foundling on someone else's doorstep. The promise is yours for life, and for life God's strength and provision are available for you to walk in that promise.

Are you pregnant with the promise of God? Rejoice, as Mary rejoiced, and know that no matter what the cost of that promise may be, either in the pregnancy or throughout the life of the child which is born, God is able to keep you through it, and the promise is worth the pain.

PRESTIDIGITATION

A Short Story

"No!" The woman thumped her hand on the table. "No! No! No! I absolutely can't accept that!"

Janet, the older cult member, smiled sweetly. "That's all right, Mrs James," she replied softly. "We respect your beliefs. We don't want to force anything upon you that you don't want to accept."

Swiftly, smoothly, ever-so-subtly, she steered the conversation onto another, non-controversial topic. Mrs James quickly regained her composure, and they chatted amicably for another ten minutes or so before the two visitors took their leave, being sure to first confirm their appointment for the study next week.

Through it all, Norman, Mrs James' 14-year-old son, curled in the armchair in the far corner of the room, ostensibly reading a comic book.

As the pair climbed into their car to move to their next appointment, Lois, the junior of the two, looked at Janet quizzically. Lois was still very new to this whole thing, and there was much that she didn't understand.

"You let her off the hook very lightly," she said, turning the statement into a question by the inflection of her voice. "Why didn't you push for her to see what you were telling her was the truth?"

"No need to push," smiled Janet. "That's why we do this as a series of studies, rather than a single hit. People need time to get used to new ideas. She will think about it through the week, and by the time we come next week it will not be a problem for her. You just watch and see!"

Sure enough, that was what happened. Their study the next week covered much of the same ground as the first week, but much more quickly. The contested question was subsumed under the heading of "the things we have already looked at", and it slipped past Mrs James without so much as a murmur from her.

It was not long, though, before something else came up that she simply could not accept. Again she banged the table. "No! No! No! That's not right at all!" Again Janet skillfully diffused the situation, turned the conversation to the innocuous, and had Mrs James eating out of her hand by the time they were ready to leave.

Again Norman listened from behind his comic book.

So it went. Week followed week; at each successive study Mrs James would compliantly accept the very things against which she had reacted strongly the week before. Each week the point would come where she would bang the table and declare that she could never accept what her visitors were saying, and each week Janet would steer the conversation in another direction, knowing that the following week they would move past this point with no problems.

Each week Norman curled in his chair, his ears carefully tuned to the conversation at the table. He knew nothing of these things, and in spite of his teenage years was still happy to follow the direction of his mother.

Finally a week came when there was no thump on the table, no cry of resistance. Carefully, Janet led Mrs James back over all the things they had covered in their study. At every point she confirmed that, yes, she understood and accepted what they were saying.

"Well," said Janet finally, feeling very pleased with her efforts. "There is just one thing left. Would you like to make a public commitment to these things that you believe, and become part of our organisation?"

"Yes," Mrs James replied eagerly. "You have taught me a great deal, and I would like to be baptised into your church."

Janet hesitated a moment. "We don't actually call ourselves a church," she said. "As you have seen through our study, the churches are totally wrong in so many of the things they teach. We don't want to be associated with them. We simply refer to ourselves as an organisation." This was a touchy part, and she whispered a silent prayer that it would not undo all that she had achieved over these weeks.

"Of course. How silly of me. I still have such a lot to learn, but I do want to be baptised."

Silently, Janet breathed a sigh of relief. Then Norman stuck his head out from the comic and asked, "Can I be baptised, too?"

So Mrs James and Norman became active members of the cult. Soon they, too, were spending many hours a week knocking on doors to share their message with anyone who would give them a hearing.

Years passed, and Norman met a delightful young girl within the cult. They married and began a family, still totally committed to the cult and its teachings, still spending hours each week spreading the message. At the same time they worked hard to save money for the Great Australian Dream, a home of their own.

Eventually they had a deposit, but not enough for a home in the area where they had been living. They would need to move to the other side of town. It was a good time to move to a new neighbourhood: their eldest son, Garry, was just about to start school, so by moving now his schooling would not be interrupted. A new neighbourhood would also mean fresh people with whom they could share their faith.

They did not have to wait long to meet their new neighbours. The furniture van had barely left when there was a knock at the door.

"Hi, I'm Susan from next door." A wave of her hand indicated which property she meant. "I won't stay, because I'm sure you have lots to do, but I thought you might like some afternoon tea. You can drop the plate back when you've settled in a bit."

Touched by her kindness, they thanked her profusely. To themselves, they wondered whether the offer of friendship would last. Most people, as soon as they learned that they were cult members, gave them a very wide berth.

Susan and her husband Peter proved to be different. Norman and Beryl soon learned that their neighbours were born-again Christians, but it made no difference to the warmth with which they were welcomed each time they visited. Norman soon learned that, except for his faith, he and Peter had a great deal in common. They began to spend considerable time together labouring over various carpentry projects, or talking about the merits of bee keeping.

Norman decided it was time to share his faith with his new-found friend. When he shared a point, Peter pulled out his battered old Bible and looked up the verse that Norman had quoted. "You know, Norm, that's really interesting. But look what it says here in the verse after it. In fact, if you read the whole chapter it is saying something very different from what you are getting from that verse." Peter gave him a Bible to take home and read for himself. He explained that the cult version may have things slightly different.

Norman was not a scholar by any means, but he took the Bible and read the whole chapter, as Peter had suggested. He was right. It seemed to be saying something very different from what he had been taught in the cult. Then he took out the cult version of the Bible and read it. Even it was saying something different when you read the whole context.

That weekend the family was visiting his mother. He told her about the conversation with Peter, and showed her the chapter in question.

"You know," his mother finally responded, looking at him with a mixture of comprehension and puzzlement, "all those years ago when those two women were taking me through the study of our faith, I felt in my heart that this was not right, but I didn't know why. I accepted what they said, but now I see it here, I guess I was right all along. On this one point, our teachers have it wrong."

It was just the first of many conversations with Peter. Each time he would listen to Norman's arguments, then take his old Bible and put the "proof" verses in context. Norman would go home, read the whole chapter, compare it with the cult Bible, and conclude for himself that the cult teaching was wrong. Then he would go and share with his mother, and she too would see the truth. The more they saw the truth, the less they were willing to go door to door sharing the cult's doctrine.

Gradually, they could feel the cords of darkness and deception uncoiling from around them, till finally one day they looked at each other and said, "No more."

"This organisation has lied to us from the word go," Norman declared. "They have deceived us and fed us half truths. What's worse, they have persuaded us that we should convince others of those lies and half truths. I can no longer be part of this." His mother and wife agreed wholeheartedly.

Peter and Susan had invited them for a barbeque that night, and as soon as Norman and Beryl walked in they knew something was different. "We are making a break with the cult," Norman announced. "We want to know how to be born again."

Delighted, their hosts shared with them the way of salvation, and they responded joyfully. Later as they talked around the coffee and pavlova, Norm shared about those long-ago meetings when his mother would thump the table.

"How on earth were we sucked into believing that stuff," he puzzled.

"Prestidigitation," replied Peter.

"Presti what?" Norman echoed.

"Prestidigitation. Slight of hand. The same technique used by stage magicians. They keep you focused on one thing, so that you won't see what else they are doing. The cult focuses on just one verse, and you don't see the big picture of what the Word is saying. The only reason they can get away with it is that people don't know what the Bible really says. Hosea tells us that people are destroyed for lack of knowledge, and it's just so true. Just look at you guys. You had faith of a kind when you started out. You believed in God, but you really didn't know anything about Him. And you were basically good people. You wanted to do the right thing, to do what God wanted. But because you didn't know the truth, you were sitting ducks for someone to come and convince you of all their garbage."

"You know, you're so right," Norman nodded. At that moment he knew that he must devote the rest of his life to making sure that others had the knowledge of the truth that alone could save them from such deception.

SET APART

As they served the Lord and fasted, the Holy Spirit said, "Separate Barnabas and Saul for me, for the work to which I have called them. (Acts 13:2)

I have known the call of God on my life since I was 12 years old, although it was not until I was 24 that I came to know the God Whose call is upon my life, and to begin to move into that call. Even at 12, when I first came to know that God was real, even though I knew nothing about Him or about the salvation that He offered me in Jesus Christ, I knew that somehow I was set apart for Himself and His service.

So it might seem a little strange that, after many years as a preacher, this verse should jump out, grab me by the ears and shake me. Yet as I read it again tonight, the force of those two words, "set apart", struck me.

Unfortunately the church today tries to be egalitarian. It emphasises the equality we have as believers, whilst ignoring the distinctions, and tries to put everybody at the same level. Or it tries to create false distinctions on the basis of race, social standing or gender - the very things which God has said are not a basis of distinction in His Kingdom. They cannot be, for they are natural and physical attributes which have no value or place in the realm of the spirit.

The truth is, we are not all the same, but what makes the difference is not any natural factor but one thing only: God's call. God's call sets some apart from the rest. It places them in a different arena, with different ground rules.

It has always been so. When God called the nation of Israel,

He set them apart from the other nations. They could not live as the nations did, but were to come under the rule of God. When God established the Old Covenant priesthood, He set them apart. The priests wore a headpiece inscribed "Holy to the Lord" - literally, "for God's use only!"

When God calls us to salvation in Christ, He sets us apart. He brings us out of the kingdom of darkness and into the Kingdom of light. He places us in a new arena, with new ground rules. We may still operate within the world, but we can no longer be part of it.

Likewise, those who are called to leadership within the Body of Christ are set apart. Now it's true that all Christians have a ministry - there can be no spectators in God's Church. It is also true that all are priests - all have access to the Throne of God, and all are called to represent Him before man and man before Him. However, not all are called to leadership. Not all are called to government. Those churches that practice congregational government on the basis of the priesthood of all believers have a great misunderstanding of that priesthood. God's Word makes it very clear that He calls some to particular places of ministry, leadership and government within the Body. And those whom He calls, He sets apart.

That does not mean that those called and set apart by God are better than the rest of the Body of Christ, nor does it mean that they are called because anything in them merited that call. If you are called to leadership, it is because God is great, not because you are great. I often tell those who believe they are called as apostles or prophets, "Don't get up on your high horse. God could just as easily have called you to be the janitor!" In fact, sometimes God delights to demonstrate His greatness by calling the least, the most unqualified, the most unlikely, and then proceeding to use them in ways that neither they nor anyone who knew them would ever have imagined.

What it does mean is that, if you are called to leadership, you cannot live as if you were not. You are set apart. You are standing on different ground. The rules for you are different. You cannot measure yourself by the rest of mankind - or even by the rest of the Church. Even when you do the same things as others, you must do them with a different motivation, a different focus.

When God set you apart, He anointed you, and whether you recognise it or not - for that matter, whether you like it or not - everything you do is touched by that anointing. Therefore, in everything you do you need to ask yourself, "Is this something upon which I can legitimately place the anointing of God?" If it is not, then you have no place doing it.

For those not called to leadership, you need to recognise that your leader is set apart. He or she carries a different burden from yours, and there will be times when he or she will see things differently, and will act differently. Support your leader. Encourage him. Pray for her. Understand that his or her separation unto the call of God is not intended to demean you, but to lift you up and release you into your own call in God. God set your leader apart before He ever created him. But just as the church at Antioch, you must also set her apart. Only then will he or she have the liberty to fulfil God's call.

SUBSTITUTE

It should have been I
in the judgement hall
facing the charges brought:
indicted justly for my wrongs
before a righteous Judge.
Yet You stood, instead,
the sinless God
hauled for judgement
before sinful man.
You spoke not
to defend Your innocence
but in silence bore my guilt
and in my place
received the sentence due to me.

It should have been I
whose back was whipped
for beatings
are for the backs of fools,
and I in foolishness
have set before You other gods
of stone, of flesh, of thought,
but mostly of myself,
whilst You
wisdom personified
have brought the truth.

It should have been I
whose hands and feet were nailed
to cruel beams
wrenched
as they shuddered into place

and torn
by the weight of sin's burden.
For my hands
have often been
the instrument of evil
and yet more often still have failed
to do the good they could have wrought;
my feet have carried me
to places where Your Spirit
could not comfortably rest.
But your hands
brought only life
and Your feet
led you only in the Father's paths.

It should have been I
whose head was crowned with angry thorns
for thoughts of anger
hatred, envy, lust and greed
are not strangers to its paths
and my mind
in rebellion
has often sought
to raise itself above the throne of God.
But Your mind bowed
before the Father's will
obedient even
to this ignominious end.

It should have been I
whose heart was pierced
this heart in which
the depths of degradation lurk;
whose motives all
are tainted with corruption
and whose purest thoughts

stink of death.
Instead, Your heart of love
was rent
not by the soldier's sword
but by my guilt.

It should have been I
who died
exposed in naked shame
before the eyes of all
who cared to look;
screaming eternally
to unresponding infinity
for the just God
who turned His head away.
But You,
the righteous One
received my wages due
and I
walking free and clean
offer my inadequate response:
Thank You.
Thank you.

THE CAMEL'S NOSE PRINCIPLE

A Modern Parable

(This article was originally published in Australia in On Being magazine in April 1989, and was reprinted in Singapore in Impact magazine in October/November 1989, under the name Lynn Cox)

It was a cold night in the desert, as most desert nights are, but Ahab the Arab was not concerned.

He was quite comfortable in his tent, with its waterproof goats hair outer covering (not that it often needed to be waterproof out there!) and its rich tapestry hangings lining the walls and ceiling. The desert sand of the floor was covered with a thick carpet, over which were strewn huge, soft cushions.

Ahab was curled up on these, his blankets pulled about him, when he felt a slight draught from the direction of the tent door. Funny, he thought, for the double flap was heavy enough to keep out even the strongest desert winds.

Turning, he saw in the flickering light of his lamp that something was intruding through the tent door. What was it?

Unable to discern the shape, he reluctantly threw back his blankets, and dragging himself from the comfort of his cushions, padded over to take a look.

As he came near the door, he suddenly realized what it was: a nose! A camel's nose, to be precise!

Ahab was cranky enough at having been forced to leave his bed: now he was really mad. He slapped the camel hard about the nose several times, all the while yelling at the top of his voice, "You mangy camel! You flea-bitten son of a desert dog! Who do you think you are? How dare you stick your nose in my tent? Get out! Get out! GET OUT! Back to the dunes where you belong!"

The camel shook his nose sharply to escape the slaps, then spoke in a low, pleading drone.

"Please, Master," he drawled, "have mercy. You are comfortable here in you tent, but the desert night outside is freezing. It is so cold that my poor nose is developing chilblains!

"I knew that you are a good, kind master, and that you would not wish your poor, faithful camel to suffer in this way, so I was sure that you wouldn't mind me sticking my nose in here where it can be warm. Please, Master, it's just my nose! It will take up such little space! Please, Master!"

The camel was making Ahab feel bad. Besides, it was late, he was tired, and his bed was beckoning him. He really didn't feel like arguing with a determined camel.

"Oh, all right," he grumbled. "I suppose just your nose won't hurt. But just your nose! Nothing more! Is that clear?"

"Of course, Master. Thank you so much. You are indeed a wonderful Master."

"Hrmph!" grunted Ahab as he shuffled back to bed.

Just as the mists of sleep were beginning to swirl about his mind, he felt it again. He raised one arm out of the blankets to be sure.

Yes, there was that slight draught coming from the tent door again. Groaning, he rolled over and looked toward the door.

This time he didn't need to get closer to see what it was – the camel's whole head was sticking through the flap. Springing out of bed, her rushed to the door and began to buffet the camel around the head.

"You lousy bag of jackal food! Didn't I tell you, your nose and nothing else? Didn't you agree to that? How is it that now your whole head is in my tent? Don't you know that your nose is just the part on the end of your head? Out, fleabag, out!"

"Oh dear, kind Master," pleaded the camel. "Surely you would not deny your faithful servant this one thing!

"You see, Master, my ears are very sensitive, particularly the tips. And the desert night is so cold! They were really burning with the cold, Master! In fact, they were in grave danger of falling off! It would not be good for my master to be seen riding a camel with no ears!

"In your great kindness, Master, let me keep my head in the tent!"

"Oh, all right," muttered Ahab, unable to think of anything to say in reply. "But just your head, hear me! Nothing else!" He turned and stomped back to bed.

Not a great length of time had passed before Ahab felt that slight draught. With a sigh, he again lifted his head and looked toward the door.

Sure enough, there was the camel with his front legs inside the tent.

Ahab jumped up and ran to the door, where he kicked the camel hard in the shins. However, he had forgotten that he had bare feet, and it hurt his toes far more than the camel's leg.

After hopping about on one foot for several minutes, he turned on the camel.

"You vermin-infested apology for a beast! Is this you head? I told you, nothing but your head! And now your legs are inside my tent! Get out, before I use your hide as a rug for the new camel I shall buy!"

"Wait, Master. Do not let your anger hide your kindness, for you are a good master who would not wish his faithful servant to suffer. You see, Master, it's my knees. I have arthritis, you know, and this cold does effect them so. Sometimes it gets so I can hardly bend.

"My master would not want his faithful camel to be unable to kneel for him to climb aboard. So I knew that my master would not mind me keeping my knees warm in his tent."

Ahab spluttered and fumed, but finally agreed. "Very well, but just your legs. Hear me, you no-good camel! Just your legs!"

Time passed, and Ahab was again drifting into sleep when again the draught came – this time a little stronger. Without even looking first, Ahab staggered to the door, where the camel was standing with his hump inside.

He didn't bother hitting or berating the camel this time, but simply stood with his hands on his hips.

"These four times you have disobeyed me, camel. What is it

this time?"

"Well, most good and kind master, it's my hump, you see. As you well know, Master, my hump holds many days' supply of water, and in the cold of this desert night it has turned to ice. Have you any idea, Master, what it feels like to have a hump full of ice?

"I knew my good master would not wish this for his faithful servant and companion....."

"All right, all right, ALL RIGHT!" sighed Ahab, cutting him short. "But not one centimetre more! I mean it this time, camel. If you disturb me again, and I find any more of you in this tent, I will take my faithful sword and slit your no-good throat from one flea-bitten ear to the other."

Quite some time passed without disturbance, and Ahab sank into a deep sleep. Then he began feeling cold. Really cold.

This was far more than a draught from the door. He tried to pull the blankets closer around him, but there were no blankets. When he reached down and patted around to find them, his hands met not the smooth plumpness of his cushions, but rough, cold sand.

His eyes sprang open. Above him was not the dark warmth of his tapestries softly lit by the flickering of his lamp, but a black sky studded with millions of stars.

He looked around. He was lying, minus both cushions and coverings, in the open desert. Some metres away he could see his tent.

Picking himself up, he hurried to the door and peered through the opening. There, lounging on his cushions and covered by his blankets, was the camel.

He had just enough time to take in the scene before two large hooves hit him squarely in the chest, sending him flying back out into the desert

As the sand settled around him, he heard a hoarse, mocking voice from the tent: "AND STAY OUT!"

For too many years, the devil has used the Camel's Nose Principle against the Church in every area from art to science, from music to politics, from education to public morality, and the Church has resisted him with all the effectiveness of a sleepy Ahab.

Isn't it time we reversed the process?

THE CHALLENGE

When I talk about the excitement, the joy, the satisfaction, the sheer thrill of being a Christian, there are inevitably those who think I'm saying that it is easy, comfortable, an arm-chair ride. It is not!

In fact, I know of nothing which could be truly described as both easy and exciting. Nothing can be comfortable and thrilling at the same time. An armchair may be cosy, but exciting? Never!

Think of the most exciting possible endeavours in the physical realm: climb a mountain, ride a wave, shoot the rapids, fly a hang-glider. None of them is easy. All require discipline, dedication. But what a thrill! What excitement!

Think of man's greatest achievements in the mental realm – art, music, literature, drama. Is it easy to paint a masterpiece or compose a symphony? Of course not! Is it satisfying? Is it exciting? It most certainly is!

Take that excitement, that satisfaction, and multiply it about a million times, and you will begin to see what the Christian life can be.

Now I'm not talking about the pew-warming variety of Christianity. There are many people who keep the church seats warm for an hour or so each Sunday, who wouldn't have the slightest idea what I'm talking about. Some of them have never come to know Jesus – they just go as a social ritual. Others know Him as Saviour, but have never realized what they have in Him, so they are comfortable – but never excited. That is not what God wants for you! I'm not talking about comfortable, pew-warming churchianity. I'm talking about total, whole-hearted, sold-out commitment tot he living Jesus Christ who can take your life and turn it upside down and place it in a completely new dimension.

It isn't easy! It isn't comfortable! Jesus never said it would be easy. In fact He said it would involve a cross to be carried every day. He said it would involve denial of self. It would involve holding lightly to all our dearest treasures, being willing to let them go.

What then must you do? Run out and buy a hair shirt? Find a good recipe for locusts and honey? Strive to do everything right? Go about with a long face? No, no, no! For Christianity from start to finish is not what you do, but what Jesus has done for you and the Holy Spirit can do in and through you.

Jesus died in your place to pay for your sin. In place of the death you deserve (as do I) He gives you life. Your part is to turn from the sin that caused that death and accept Jesus and the gift He gives you.

If you have done that you are a Christian. That's a great start! But don't let it stop there! Don't get comfortable! God has so much more to do in your life yet. He wants to lead you into the kind of exciting life I have been talking about. And He will, if you will let Him.

Your part is surrender. That may sound easy, but let me assure you, it isn't. The hardest thing I have ever learned – and am still learning – to do is surrender. There is so much of me that wants to hang onto my life, to keep control. Yet as I yield that control to the Holy Spirit, I find that He is opening up new worlds to me every day. Yes, there is a cross, and it hurts – don't come to Jesus asking for the cross experience and expect to feel no pain. The whip on Jesus' back, the thorns on His head, the nails in His hands and feet all hurt; but without them there would never have been the victory of Easter morning!

If you will surrender to the Holy Spirit and allow Him to work the cross in your life, you too will find a victory, a triumph which makes the cross not only acceptable but desirable.

No, this experience of Jesus is not easy, nor comfortable. There is discipline. Sometimes there is pain. Always there is a cross. But there is a joy which transcends every pain. There is victory and triumph and excitement. I would not want any other kind of life! Would you?

THE GODS WE CREATE

Some awesome things had been happening in the last few months. After 450 years in Egypt, during the latter half of which they had degenerated from being honoured guests as the people of Prime Minister Joseph, to being despised slaves, the people of Israel had seen Moses raised up as their deliverer. Suddenly the God of whom they had only heard through the stories of their elders had shown Himself to be real, and what's more to be interested in them. Moses, who 40 years earlier had tried to deliver them in his own strength and as a result of his abysmal failure had fled into self-imposed exile in the desert, had returned saying that God had told him to set them free. More than that, he had backed his claims with some pretty impressive miracles – so much so that, after the first couple, the magicians of Egypt gave up even trying to emulate them. Finally, after declaring that the every firstborn male in Egypt would be killed, except for those of the Israelites who gathered in homes where the blood of a lamb had been placed on the door frame, he had led them out of Egypt.

When they were gathered on the shores of the Red Sea and the Egyptians, having changed their minds about letting their slaves get away, were bearing down on them, Moses raised his staff over the sea and the waters parted to allow the Israelites to cross, then closed drowning the pursuing Egyptians. From there, he led them to Mt Sinai, where they watched in terror as the mountain quaked and shuddered under the power of God, and its summit was shrouded with smoke and fire. No way were they going up there! They had been very happy to suggest that Moses should go up and talk to God on their behalf.

It had all been very impressive, very awesome. One would

think that there would be no way that any one of those two-million-odd people could possibly doubt the reality of their God.

Yet now, nearly six weeks after Moses disappeared into the smoke and fire, they had decided that he had vanished off the face of the earth, and therefore they had best do something. So they called on Moses assistant, Brother Aaron, and asked him to produce a more manageable substitute for the awesome God who had revealed Himself to them over recent months.

"Come, make us gods which shall go before us," they said (Ex. 32:1). What they wanted was a figurehead, not a sovereign Lord. They wanted a god who would take them where they wanted to go, rather than one who would lead them in paths of His own choosing, and insist that they not only follow Him, but move when He moved and stop when He stopped.

Aaron told them to take off their gold earrings and give them to them. This was to be a god which owed its very existence to them, and was totally dependent on their generosity. Such a god would always be subservient to them. One who needed them so much could never be in a position to make demands of them. They were not interested in the God to whom they owed their very existence, and upon whose mercy they were dependent every moment. They had no use for a God who didn't need them, who could say, "I have no need for a bull from your stall, nor male goats from your pens. For every animal of the forest is mine, and the livestock on a thousand hills. " (Ps. 50:9-10). Such a God was far too big for them, and reminded them far too easily of their own insignificance.

So Aaron made the idol, casting and shaping it into a calf. The people wanted a god made in their image, according to their pattern; one they could shape as they pleased. They were not interested to know that they were made in the image of the true

God, and that they were supposed to reflect that image to the world around them.

When the image was complete, Aaron declared that the next day would be "a festival to the Lord." Whilst Moses was up the mountain receiving from God His commands for His people, what the people wanted was a god whose only command was to celebrate.

How foolish were the Israelites, we think! Yet, I wonder, have we ever sought to create a god who was just a little more comfortable, just a little more manageable, than the God of the Bible? Have we ever tried to make a god who would take us where we wanted to go, whilst making us look good as his faithful followers? Have we ever sought to make God dependent on us, rather than acknowledging our dependence on Him? Have we ever tried to create Him in our image, rather than accepting His image in us, and allowing Him to conform us to His image? Have we ever wanted a god whose only command was to have a great big party?

In many cases, our lives and even our worship suggest that is exactly the kind of god we worship. Sadly, gods of our own creation are as helpless as the calf produced by Aaron. They have no power to save us, no power to transform us, no power to help us in any way.

Far better, then, to grind the gods of our own creation to dust, and turn back to the God of the Bible, the God who manifested Himself in the person of the Lord Jesus Christ.

TOGETHER IN THE STORM

It was a time of turmoil in the land. The warnings of the prophets over hundreds of years, calling the nation to forsake its idols and turn back to the Lord in repentance, had largely fallen on deaf ears. The good king, Josiah, had brought about massive reforms, tearing down the idolatrous altars and restoring the feast of Passover, but his reforms did not outlive him. His son, Jehoahaz, quickly turned back to the evil ways of earlier kings. As a result God allowed Pharaoh to raid the land and take Jehoahaz captive, installing his brother Eliakim as a puppet king and changing his name to Jehoiakim. As a result, Jehoiakim taxed the people heavily in order to pay the tribute imposed upon him by Pharaoh.

At the same time, raiding parties from all the surrounding nations were coming against Judah, intent on destroying it. Worst of all, Babylon was looming, and quickly stepped in taking large numbers of the people captive.

Through all this, Jeremiah was prophesying against the nation, and his scribe Baruch was often the one responsible for delivering those messages of God's judgement. Baruch, it seems, was not terribly impressed with this whole scenario. He was suffering, and he was complaining about it.

Then the Lord gave Jeremiah a word to give to Baruch, not to take to others but for himself. "You shall tell him, Yahweh says: 'Behold, that which I have built, I will break down, and that which I have planted I will pluck up; and this in the whole land. Do you seek great things for yourself? Don't seek them; for, behold, I will bring evil on all flesh,' says Yahweh; 'but I will let you escape with your life wherever you go.' " (Jer 45:4-5)

In simple, modern terms, God said, "Baruch, stop whinging! You are in this storm with the rest of the world, and it's My doing."

As I read this passage in the middle of yet another lockdown, with businesses collapsing all around, with fear rampant through the community, with the spectre of hopelessness everywhere, I couldn't help but think how relevant this is to our lives today.

Whether it is a virus, or some natural disaster, or something else that impacts our whole nation, we are all in the same storm. And whether or not you believe that all this is a direct judgement of God against a world that is even more rebellious against Him than was Judah in the days of Jeremiah, we can at least say that God has allowed it.

The big question is, what will be our response?

Do we, like Baruch, complain about the effects that all this is having on us personally? Do we whine because of the restrictions and frustration? Grizzle about the sheer injustice of it all?

Or will we look beyond our own discomfort and take it as an opportunity for intercession? Will we rejoice that the Church is being pushed into prayer like never before? That there is a sifting and purifying taking place from which the Bride will emerge in radiant glory?

We are all together in the storm. The choice we have to make is whether we will allow the storm to beat us down and destroy us, or whether we will rise above it and come through in victory.

THE KING'S FRIEND

The kings of the ancient world were prone to gather officials around them, with each one being responsible for some part of the royal household or the administration of the kingdom. David was no exception to this rule, and 1 Chronicles 27:25-34 gives a detailed list of some of these officials and their specific duties. Right at the end there is a little part of a verse that always makes me smile. After naming numerous people, each of whom "was in charge of...." there is the simple statement, "Hushai was the king's friend." What an important friendship that must have been, to be listed alongside all the officials and their official duties.

When I read this, I think about Abraham who was called God's friend. This was not in any sense a diminishing of Abraham's importance or that of the things he did. Abraham was a great man of God, so much so that the Bible speaks of him as the father of the faithful. To God, however, the most important thing about Abraham was that he was His friend.

Have you ever thought about what it means to be a friend to God, as opposed to simply being one of His servants, or even one of His "officials"? A servant may respect his master. He may be faithful in carrying out the duties which his master requires of him, and even going above and beyond the call of duty. He may even have a sincere affection for his master, and genuinely desire to see his master's interests prosper. Yet no matter how much respect or affection there is, there can never be the kind of intimacy that comes with friendship. There is always a distance between the servant and the master, a level of formality which prevents either from sharing too closely or becoming too deeply involved.

Friendship is different. True friends are open with each other, sharing from the heart. In a mature friendship there is an intimacy which means that many things don't even need to be articulated, because each simply understands the other's thought patterns. Even if there are differences in the socio-economic standing of the two friends, those differences do not form a barrier or create a formality between them.

True friends are there for each other. They enjoy each other's company, and they are available to lend a sympathetic ear or a shoulder to cry on, as well as to shout and rejoice with their friend when things go well, or simply to laugh together and enjoy the pleasures of life. Friends share. They share experiences, both the joyful and the sorrowful. They share time. They share possessions. Most of all they share their heart.

How important it must have been for David the king to have such a friend – someone who was not there to demand anything from him, who was not seeking position and prestige, but who simply liked him and enjoyed his company, and was willing to listen when he needed to sound off about life.

How important it must be also to God to have friends. Unlike people, He doesn't need friends – He is perfect, which means He is complete in Himself and needs nothing added to Him. However, I am sure He delights to find people who simply love Him for Himself, people who are not all the time demanding or trying to juggle for position in the kingdom but who just want to be in His presence and to enjoy His company. No wonder Jesus was upset when James and John tried to preempt the other disciples and have Jesus declare that they were to sit at His right and left in the kingdom. He had chosen them as two of His three closest followers, had shared with them a degree of intimacy which should have placed them among His best friends, but by this action they showed that they were in fact not friends at all, but merely courtiers.

Let's seek to develop a friendship with God. Instead of worrying all the time about our work for Him, or striving for personal promotion, let's focus on who He is, and get to know Him. Let's develop a love of being in His company – not always for the deep intercession or the soaring worship, though of course these are wonderful, but at times simply "hanging out" with Him, chatting about the ordinary things around us, and developing a sense of His presence wherever we may be and whatever He may be doing. Let's make our ears available for God to talk to us – not necessarily to give us great earth-shattering messages for others, but simply to share His heart with us. Have you ever heard God say concerning the things around you, "That delights Me," or "That saddens Me"? A friend would, because that's how friends share. Have you ever said as you looked at a beautiful sunset, "Lord, You did a really good job painting that!" or as you sank into a hot bath, "Lord, thank You for giving man the intelligence to put heat and water together!" or, while struggling with an unobliging sewing machine, "Jesus, why couldn't You have been a dressmaker instead of a carpenter?" These are the kind of things that friends share – ordinary yet intimate.

Of course, being God's friend does not mean that we lose our reverence for Him, or our awe of Him. Whilst maintaining these, however, God is calling us into a relationship of intimacy. Personally, I think it would be nice if when the books are written up they say, "So-and-so was in charge of this, and Such-and-such was in charge of that, and Lynn was God's friend."

WHAT DOES REVIVAL LOOK LIKE?

Here in Victoria we recently had the massive Awakening Australia rallies. It is exciting for Christians to gather with thousands of others of like mind to worship Jesus, and it is wonderful that many of those who attended the rallies went out into the streets to share the Gospel. Yet I find myself wondering, is this what revival is about? What would a true revival look like?

I believe the first manifestation of a true revival is a renewed awareness of the holiness of God. Yes, He is our loving Daddy, and calls us into an intimate relationship with Himself; but He is also the mighty King and Ruler of the universe who is perfect in every aspect. Not only is He holy, but He calls us to be holy. True revival brings a revelation of His holiness, and with it a desperate hunger for His holiness to be manifested through our own lives.

That revelation of holiness stirs profound and sincere repentance. Repentance for our personal sin; repentance for the sin of the Church, of which we are a part; repentance for the sin of our nation, which we represent. Repentance that is not only an expression of sorrow, but a longing and a willingness for transformation.

Revival brings a renewed alignment with and passion for the Word of God. The standards of God's Word can no longer be dismissed as irrelevant, or subjected to our own opinions of right and wrong. There is a divine turn about in our thinking as that which was upside down and inside out is turned right way. The Bible is no longer left on the shelf, or read only as a duty to be performed as quickly as possible. Rather it is devoured by hearts hungry to squeeze out every last drop, to find every hidden nugget of truth, and to apply it to our lives.

With revival comes a hunger for the presence of God. Prayer meetings overflow. Worship bursts out of the time limits normally imposed upon it. Other activities become irrelevant as God's people just want to be in His presence.

Then something else begins to happen. As God's people allow Him to draw them more and more to Himself, and transform them more and more into His likeness, they find that they are also sharing His heart for the world. We begin to be filled with His compassion. Christianity is no longer about having our own needs met. Rather it is about laying down our lives so that we might take the love of God to a dying world. Intercession becomes intense as we take hold of the power of God in one hand and the need of mankind in the other, and bring them together. Then our prayers grow legs and carry us out to meet that need.

Then, by the power of the Spirit of the living God, we will turn the world upside down - or, rather, right way up.

THE OTHER SIDE OF DEATH

I believe it was Deitrich Bonhoffer who said, "When Christ calls a man He bids him, 'Come and die'." Jesus said that we must be willing to take up our cross on a daily basis; and that by losing our lives we save them, but if we attempt to save them we will lose them. Paul wrote, "I have been crucified with Christ."

Certainly some are called to martyrdom, a crown which both Bonhoffer and Paul ultimately received, but is that all these statements were about? Is the death of which they speak purely physical? Can the rest of us, who may never have to face the extreme test of our faith, happily ignore such sentiments?

In fact all of them were talking about a different level of death - a level which we all have to enter if we want to experience the fullness that is available in our Christian walk, and without which physical martyrdom is not only meaningless but impossible.

Paul, writing in Galatians 2:20, speaks of death in three areas. Firstly, as he writes to those who want to return to living under the Law, he declares that he is dead to the Law. When Christ died in fulfilment of the Law, he reasons, He was totally identified with Paul. Christ died in Paul's place, as Paul, to the extent that it was as if Paul had died. Since the Law cannot have any power over a dead man, it no longer has any authority over Paul. He is dead to the Law. This gives weight to his whole argument that no-one is justified by observing the Law: how can anyone be justified by observing that which has no power over him, and to which he is dead?

Secondly, Paul is dead to sin. Just as the Law can have no

power over a dead man, neither can sin. When it comes to sin, everyone is dead. There are two options: either we are dead in sin, or we are dead to sin in Christ. Paul's point is that those who are dead to sin cannot continue to live in sin.

Thirdly, Paul is dead to Paul. "I no longer live" goes far beyond his legal standing in Christ to reflect his experiential position. Paul has been to the cross. He has experienced the crushing that is "death to self."

Some Christians talk about dying to self as if they were going on a picnic, but the reality is that this death is every bit as grim and painful as any physical martyrdom. Our own ideas, our own priorities and agendas, our own strengths and abilities, our own self righteousness must be brought to nothing if we are to truly live the Christian life in the way God intended. The process can be agony: a black hell from which we feel there will never be an escape. We watch everything we thought we had being stripped from us, see ourselves become totally incompetent in the areas where we felt we had it most together, and in the midst of it all wonder why God seems to have retreated to the farthest corner of the universe - or perhaps even of some other universe far, far away from this one.

Of course, many Christians will never experience this. They are content to live at a far more comfortable level. For those who want the full reality of life in Christ, however, the crushing, the breaking, the death is inevitable and necessary. Jesus could have come down from the Cross. He could have said, "No, I don't want this. I want to live a long and happy and profitable life, and I want to die in comfortable old age with my family and friends around me." Had He done so, He would have lost His destiny.

Paul experienced that breaking in the three years following his

Damascus Road experience, when he drew aside to learn from the Lord. Imagine what a crushing blow it would be to learn that everything you have believed for your entire life - or at least your interpretation of it - has been wrong. Imagine the breaking that would come with the discovery that your impassioned efforts to defend the Name of your God had in fact been directed against Him. Imagine the devastation that would accompany the revelation that all the righteousness in which you had so prided yourself was nothing more than filthy rags: worse, that instead of bringing you closer to God as you had imagined, it had in fact led you away from Him to such a point that you could now see yourself as "the worst of sinners." When Paul talked about having been crucified with Christ, he was not just using a nice, poetic expression. He had truly been to the Cross, and seen the death-blow dealt to everything that he had held dear. The truth of his heart had been laid bare, his strength exposed as weakness and his zeal as sin.

Yet for all its necessity, death is only half the story. The Cross without the resurrection would have been meaningless. Had Christ remained in the grave, He would have been just another martyr, and we would have justifiably mourned the tragedy of a promising young life cut short. It is the resurrection that makes the Cross a victory.

So, for us, the breaking is essential, but not as an end in itself. Many have been broken and never recovered. The crushing has destroyed them, broken their faith, destroyed spirit, soul and body, and left them as wrecks, lost to the Kingdom and to themselves. Others are transformed by the breaking, and come out the other side of it as vessels of honor, fit for the use of the King. What makes the difference? **But Christ** ... "I no longer live, **but Christ** lives in me." The only point of death to self is that we might live to Christ.

Just as the Father did not send Christ to the Cross to gain some kind of sadistic pleasure from seeing Him suffer, so He does not break us because He wants to destroy us. Rather, it is to destroy everything in us that keeps us from living in the fullness of His life. Just as we can be dead under the Law, or dead to the Law in Christ, but not both; just as we can be dead in sin or dead to sin in Christ, but not both; so we can be alive in our own life, or alive in the resurrection life of Christ, but not both.

For us to enter into that resurrection life, something has to happen that takes us beyond the breaking, beyond the death. At some point in the midst of the crushing, in the absence of God's tangible presence, in the pain and confusion of being brought to nothing, there has to be a transfer. I'm dead ... but Christ lives in me. I can no longer even summons faith ... but I live by the faith of the Son of God. I am totally destroyed ... but in Christ I rise up in victory. I can do nothing ... but I can do all things in Christ Who strengthens me.

How do we do it? It is tempting to try to reach down to some place deep, deep inside us and dredge up the last remaining shred of our strength to somehow take hold of a new level of faith. To do so is fruitless, for if we can find that last shred of strength we will only call forth yet further breaking till it, too, is destroyed.

When we get to the end of ourselves, there is only one thing to do: surrender. Jesus final prayer before His death was, "Father, into Your hands I commend my spirit." The only difference between those who are broken and destroyed and those who are broken and raised to new life is that the former refuse to let go. Stubborn to the last minute, they hold on to their lives, and in doing so lose them. Refusing to release what was theirs, they go down with the sinking ship. Jesus said that it is when we lose our lives - when we willingly surrender them into the

Father's hands to do with as He pleases, that we gain them. Only when we reach that point are we finally dead. All that has led up to it has merely been the dying process.

Knowing that, many are tempted to "easy surrender." "I surrender all," we sing; but we are not really embracing death, but rather seeking the nice feeling of being touched by God. What we really want is to pass through death quickly, without the pain, and move straight to resurrection. Unfortunately, that option is not available. The death process must do its work in us, until at last we reach that point of surrender, that point where we are dead. And it is only when we are finally dead that the Spirit who raised Christ from the dead can also give us resurrection life.

JESUS: WHAT KIND OF MAN IS THIS? (Part 1)

The disciples were completely baffled. They had set out to cross the lake in their fishing boat, but suddenly - as so often happened on this treacherous stretch of water - a violent storm sprang up, and they were fearful for both their lives and their boat. Yet when they woke Jesus, who had been calmly sleeping through the tumult, He simply spoke to the wind and waves and they were still. The disciples looked at each other. They were used to seeing His miracles, but this was something new. What kind of man was this Who had come into their lives? What kind of man can speak to wind and waves and have them obey?

They knew for a start that He was not like the religious leaders of the day. On the whole, the religious leaders - the Pharisees and Sadducees, the Scribes and priests - were men who had set themselves apart from everyone else. As guardians of the Law, the Temple and the sacrificial system, they saw themselves as vastly superior to the common rabble. They were, after all, men of learning, while the ordinary crowd knew nothing. They prided themselves in their righteousness in following the Law, whilst the common crowd was nothing but a bunch of sinners.

Yet for all their learning, for all their elitism, for all their talk, they were totally lacking in any real authority. The best they could offer when they preached was to pull together the opinions of other men, quoting this rabbi, that rabbi and some other rabbi and comparing their viewpoints in an endless discussion of empty philosophy.

And they certainly did not have any power. No-one had ever heard of a Pharisee or Sadducee healing the sick, raising the dead or calming a storm.

There were, of course, a few who were different. Nicodemus came in all sincerity to seek Jesus; Joseph gave his own tomb for the burial of Jesus' body; and Gamaliel warned the Jews who were persecuting the early Church that if this thing was of God their resistance to it would not succeed. But for the most part the religious leaders were so caught up in the form of religion that they bore absolutely no relevance to everyday life.

Jesus was the exact opposite. Far from pushing people away from Him by aloofness, He drew them like a magnet. Not just religious people. Not just good people. In fact, many of those who were most drawn to Jesus were the very ones who would have crossed to the other side of the street - or even the other side of town! - to avoid contact with the religious leaders. Tax collectors. Prostitutes. Sinners of all varieties. They were drawn by Jesus' warmth and love.

Yet He was not like them, either. He touched prostitutes, yet was never touched by even the faintest hint of immorality. He ministered to cheats, liars and thieves, yet was never less than totally, transparently honest. He dealt with the brutal and callous, yet never wavered in His own compassion and mercy.

As far as the disciples knew, Jesus had never undertaken any formal study. For the religious leaders, it was a matter of considerable pride to be able to say, "I studied at the feet of so-and-so" - particularly if "so-and-so" happened to be a widely known and highly honoured rabbi. Jesus made no such claims. Rather, He said simply, "I do what I see My Father doing. I say what I hear My Father saying."

Yet He spoke as no man had ever spoken. He did not call on the authority of other rabbis, but on His own. He dared to even override or expand upon the words of the prophets of old, and even of the Law itself. "You have heard it said ..." He told them, "... but I say unto you..." The Law had limited the extent of retribution, saying that for an eye one should take no more than an eye; but Jesus exhorted them to forgo retribution entirely, instead loving their enemies and doing good to those who harmed them. He spoke as One who had not the slightest doubt about His own authority.

What's more, His speaking was not just empty words. It was backed up with power. When He spoke to blind eyes, they opened. When He spoke to demons, they left whatever body they had been inhabiting. When He spoke to dead people, they came to life. When He spoke to raging wind and seas, they grew calm. No religious leader the disciples had ever heard of did anything like that!

Yet at the same time, Jesus was not like the ordinary people. Most of the common people knew nothing of the Law, and cared even less. Except when the religious leaders cornered them and confronted them with their religious duties, they mostly went about life their own way. For them, being Jewish was like belonging to some kind of club that made theme somehow special simply by belonging. And whilst most of the community would stand apart from those who committed great sins, very few attempted - or expected - to live a truly righteous life. After all, holiness was for the religious professionals, and they were just common folk.

Jesus, on the other hand, held the Law in high esteem. He seemed to know it, and to understand it, instinctively, even without formal training. He declared that it could not be broken. He said that not even the tiniest letter or portion of letter would be removed from it till it was fulfilled. He said that He had not come to destroy the Law, but to fulfill it.

Of course, the Pharisees accused Him of breaking the Law, particularly when it came to His insistence upon healing even on the Sabbath. After all, if people had been sick for years, surely waiting one more day was not going to harm them. But every time they brought it up, Jesus pointed to the spirit of the Law, and rebuked them for their blindness and hardness of heart.

For all His own commitment to the Law, Jesus was compassionate toward those who failed to meet its requirements. Unlike the Pharisees who flaunted their own legalistic righteousness and strongly condemned all who fell short of it, Jesus walked in true righteousness but did not condemn even the worst of sinners. Unlike the crowd, who considered the Law irrelevant and sin unimportant, He gently told those who had fallen to "go and sin no more."

The crowd saw Jewishness as little more than membership of an elite social club, but at the same time saw those who were not members as being vastly beneath them. Jesus saw Jewishness as a central, vital relationship with God, but at the same time extended to non-Jews an unheard-of level of acceptance and recognition, on several occasions honouring them above the people of His own race. He may have been a magnet for the people, but He was definitely not like them.

The disciples also knew that this man was not like themselves. As the wind and waves had beat around their small boat, threatening to capsize it, it had not even occurred to them that He would be able to still the racket with no more than a word. They had woken Him to get another pair of hands on the oars, somewhat annoyed that He would sleep through such a crisis. The only thing they could see was the size of those waves, and the looming picture of themselves gurgling to the bottom of the lake. Any hope they had of being saved was more like a fleeting wish.

Jesus did not share their fears and anxiety. It seemed as though He just didn't see the storm. He maintained absolute serenity; He was totally in control. There was no hint of struggling to summon faith, of trying to believe against the evidence of His eyes. He simply rebuked the storm, much like one would rebuke an over-boisterous child. Then He rebuked them for their lack of faith, apparently totally unsympathetic to their fears.

It was not the first time He had seen what they could not see, and behaved as they would not behave. There was the time when they had spent the entire night fishing, and met the morning with empty nets. They were professionals: they knew that this was a hopeless quest, and that any further attempt would be simply a waste of time and effort. Then along comes this carpenter - what would He know about fishing? - and says, "Put out for a catch." They knew it was utter foolishness, but they did it to humour Him - and broke their nets with fish! How did He know? How did He do that?

Then there was the centurion. Not only was this guy not a Jew, he was part of the much-hated army of occupation. Had it been any one of them that he approached, they would have told him where to go very smartly, and not spared the language in doing it. Instead, Jesus not only heard him out but offered to go with him to heal his servant. When the centurion said that was not necessary, that He was unworthy, but that he had a clear understanding of Jesus' authority, Jesus not only healed the servant from a distance but commended the Roman officer's faith as being greater than that of many Jews. No, the disciples knew, this man Jesus was definitely not like them!

What kind of man was He?

JESUS: WHAT KIND OF MAN IS THIS? (Part 2)

What kind of man is this? the disciples asked themselves, as they watched Jesus still the raging storm with no more than a couple of words. They knew He was not like their religious leaders, nor like the sinners who were so powerfully drawn to Him. He was not like the ordinary people, and not even like themselves, His disciples. What kind of man was He?

We know that He was God in the flesh, the eternal second Person of the Trinity: God the Son who took on human flesh and became the Son of God. (John 1:14) Yet His humanity was real. It was not just a pretence, a mask that He put on while He was on earth. Nor was He part God, part man, like some of the Greek and Roman demi-gods. He laid aside everything it meant to be God - all the power, all the prerogatives - and became fully man, without ever ceasing to be fully God. (Philippians 2:6-7) While He was on earth, He lived as man, not as God. Every bit of authority He had on earth, every bit of power, every miracle He performed, had its source not in His own Godhood, but in His total reliance upon the power of the Holy Spirit within Him.

He was man as God created man to be. In the beginning, God created man "in His own image and likeness" to be like Him in every way. (Genesis 1:27) Man was designed to be perfectly in tune with his Creator; reflecting both His character and His behaviour. Man was to *be* like God, so that the rest of creation could look at man and see what God was like. Man was to *act* like God, and so be a fitting vice-regent to rule over the earth as God's representative.

The first people God created failed in that mandate. Rather

than rejoicing that they were made to be like God, and to represent Him, they fell for the devil's lie that they could be "as gods" - that they could be gods for themselves, not merely representing Another, but ruling in their own right, making their own laws and setting their own standards. (Genesis 3:4) In doing so, they fatally damaged their likeness to God. Both in character and in action they became unlike Him. Their rebellion made them both unfit to be His representatives, and unable to, as their obedience to satan had made him their lord and handed dominion over the earth to him.

God, however, still intended to have a man - a human person - representing Him on earth. So Jesus came, to be the kind of man that man was meant to be: a man who was so fully like God that the rest of creation could look at Him and know what God was like. To be the kind of man who could truly say to His disciples, "He who has seen me has seen the Father." (John 14:9)

He was like God in His holiness. Even though He lived in a sinful world, and even mingled with those whom many would have considered to be the "scum of the earth", He was never tainted by sin. He was like God in His goodness, bringing blessing wherever He went, whether it was to a widow who had lost her only son (and therefore her only means of support), or to a bridal party that had simply run out of wine. He was like God in mercy and compassion, touching lepers to bring them healing and forgiving even the vilest of sinners. He was also like God in authority and power, bringing disease, demons and even death into subjection to Himself, and bringing healing, release and provision with just a few words.

"Of course He was like God," some might say. "He was God!" That misses the point. Jesus was not like God because He was God; but because, as man, He lived in total dependence upon the Holy Spirit within Him. Yes, He came to show us what

God was like; but He also came to show us what man was meant to be like. If He had lived as God, we could never hope to emulate Him, for we are not God. Because He lived as man filled with, surrendered to, and reliant up on God, He shows us that we can do the same.

Jesus was a man who showed us both what God is like, and what we can be like. But just as He represented God to us, He also represented us to God. Before our first parents sinned, God had told them clearly that the penalty for disobedience would be death: not just physical death, in which their perfect bodies would begin immediately to break down, and after many years would cease to function all together; but spiritual death, in which they would be immediately and forever cut off from the life of God. (Genesis 2:17) Death at both levels - as well as a myriad of other manifestations of death - was the portion of every person ever born from that time forward.

However, it was not God's purpose that people should die: He had not created us for death. His love wanted to see us enjoying His life in all its fullness. This raised a dilemma: how could God's justice, which demanded a penalty for sin, and His love, which desired life for the sinner, be reconciled?

God's answer was Jesus. He was the only man ever born for the specific purpose of dying. More than any other person who has ever lived, He was a man of destiny: and that destiny was a cross. A death penalty for sin had to be paid, and it had to be paid for every person who had ever lived and for every person who would ever live. That's why no ordinary man could fill this role. Every other person on earth deserved the death penalty for his or her own sins. Since each person could only die once, that made it impossible for any to bear the death penalty of another. Even if there had been one sinless person, that one could only have died for one other. To pay the penalty for all mankind required an infinite sacrifice, and only One who was Himself infinite was sufficient to make it.

Death, however, would not be the end for Him. During His life on earth He demonstrated His power over death for others: how, then, could death hold Him? He had experienced many encounters with the devil and his power whilst He was on earth, and on every occasion had been victorious. But the greatest victory was the seeming defeat of the Cross, because through it He broke the power of sin to hold mankind captive to death. Calvary marked the defeat of Satan, and Jesus became the first person ever to rise from the dead never to die again.

What kind of man was this? He was a man unlike any other. A man who perfectly manifested what God is like. A man who perfectly demonstrated what man can be like. A man who, in His own death, paid the death penalty for every person who would accept it. A man who, by defeating death, is able to offer life to everyone who will come to Him.

Will you come?

WHERE'S THE SALT?

I was in Nepal recently, before the new Parliament was appointed and voted to declare Nepal as no longer a Hindu nation, but a secular one. At that time it was still technically illegal to preach the Gospel there. One of our pastors came to me, obviously troubled. Someone had reported his evangelistic activities, and he faced the prospect of being charged, which could result in a minimum of five years in jail.

"Mom Lynn," he said, "I really don't want to go to jail!" Of course he didn't: he was pastoring a pioneer church, about to launch a Bible College, and his young wife was just weeks away from giving birth to their first child. Then he gave a little shrug, and with half a grin added, "Oh well, we don't have a prison ministry yet. If I go to jail, I guess we will!"

We praise God that when he went to the police station to answer the charge, the officer in charge was not interested. "There are men in this area," he said, "who used to spend so much time in my jail that they practically owned it. Suddenly, I did not see them for a long time. I thought they must have been killed, but then I learned that they had become Christians. If your Gospel can keep such people out of my jail, then I will not do anything to stop you preaching it."

Wherever I go in restricted nations, the story is similar. The Christians are vitally involved in their communities, regardless of the potential cost. They live their Christian faith in front of the world in such a way that the world must take notice: love them or hate them, it cannot ignore them.

By contrast, many Christians in the west seem intent upon wrapping themselves up in a comfortable cocoon of

Christianity, and touching the world as little as possible. In many places it is possible to go from cradle to grave immersed in a Christian sub-culture. Children go from a Christian education system to a Christian work place; they listen to Christian radio, watch Christian television, read Christian comics and magazines and go to Christian social groups and sporting clubs. As adults they vote for a Christian political party and attend a Christian medical practice; when they want a holiday they take a Christian tour, and when they retire the buy into a Christian retirement village.

All this may sound very comfortable, even idyllic, but at some point we must stop and ask ourselves, what is the purpose of our being in this world? Are we called to cling together in little pockets of believers, mindful only of our own survival in an increasingly hostile world?

Surely not! Jesus said that we were to be the "salt of the earth."

Now, spread properly throughout a dish, salt adds flavor and enhances the dish. But if you're happily eating a bowl of Mum's best stew and suddenly come across a lump of salt all stuck together, it not only doesn't taste very nice, it can even make you feel sick!

We may enjoy our Christian sub-culture, but is it perhaps separating us from the very people whom God has called us to reach, and alienating us from them even to the point of making them sick?

To be the "salt of the earth", three things are necessary.

Firstly, we have to be salty. The very essence of salt is that it is different. It has that quality, that tang that other food does not have. Our whole purpose in adding it to our food is to provide that which is lacking in the food itself.

Likewise, we are different – or we are supposed to be! We have the one thing that the world does not have: the very life of God within us. That means, very simply, that the nature of God should be evident in us. When people look at us, they should see what God is like.

We are called to be a "peculiar people", a people who are different from the world around us. If we are not, then we have nothing to offer. If we are just the same as the guy next door, then what can we possibly add to his life that he doesn't already have? Just as the tang of salt stands in stark contrast to the blandness of the food to which it is added, so we must stand in start contrast to the world about us.

Secondly, it is not enough for us to be salty, we must be salty in the situation. The only way we can stand in contrast to the world, is by being in the world.

Salt is absolutely useless while it stays in the salt-pot. It can be the best quality salt in the world, but it won't achieve a thing until it gets into the stew!

Likewise, we cannot be the salt of the earth unless we are spread throughout the earth.

Jesus never founded any monasteries! Of course, most of us would never consider entering a literal monastery, yet so often we build spiritual monasteries around ourselves by our exclusiveness, withdrawing from non-Christian situations to cling to Christian company.

Have we never thought that when we deliberately withdraw our Christian presence from any situation, we are in effect handing it over to the devil? If we refuse to be involved in politics, do we really have a right to complain when non-believers run our countries? If we withdraw from the education system, can we then complain that it is run by humanists? If we consider the "secular" music industry outside of our scope, can we gripe that it is under the control of the devil?

Of course, it is easy to excuse ourselves by saying that as Christians we are not given a voice in certain situations. My friends in restricted countries are not given a voice, and can potentially face severe penalties if they speak up anyway: but they speak, anyway! Even if you are not able to speak to people in the situation, you can infiltrate it and still bring a Christian influence.

Take schools for example. So, you can't pray or read the Bible at a state school. No one can stop you from meeting with other parents from that school outside of the school to pray for the school, the teachers and the students. No one can stop you from getting involved on whatever committees are available and bringing a Christian perspective to every meeting you attend. You don't have to climb on a chair and preach the Gospel, you simply have to vote "no" to anti-Christian propositions, and put forward suggestions that honour God.

Of course, you can stop yourself from doing these things, by withdrawing into the comfort of the Christian sub-culture.

Except for those which are immoral, Christians should be permeating every area of human endeavour and interest: every kind of work, every work place, every hobby or entertainment. They all need salt!

Finally, to be the salt of the earth we need to release our saltiness into the situation. The salt in Mum's stew is only effective as it "dies" to itself by dissolving into the liquid. We, too, need to "die" to our own desire to be comfortable in the constant company of those who share our faith, choosing rather to release that faith to the faithless world around us. In the example of a school, be even more involved than non-believing parents. Volunteer for canteen and other duties. Grab every opportunity to share with non-Christian parents, teachers and students – not just to preach to them, but to share your life and your Christian perspective on the day-to-day. Release your saltiness into the situation! Try similar tactics in your workplace, your neighbourhood, or wherever else you find yourself.

David du Plessis once said, "Salt makes people thirsty. If we wonder why this world isn't thirsty enough, maybe it's because we're not salty enough!"

Church! Let's "salt down" this world till we create a thirst that can only be quenched by Jesus!

WHO RAIDED THE ARK WHILE IT WAS LOST?

At last the Temple was complete. The stones had been chiselled and set in place, the wood lovingly carved, and the whole thing extravagantly overlaid with gold.

The furniture was in place. The bronze altar for the sacrifices pointed forward to the Cross, where God's ultimate sacrifice would be offered to provide not only a covering for man's sin, but total forgiveness and restoration.

The bath where the priests were to bathe before each ceremony spoke of the need to "keep short accounts" with God, coming to Him regularly to receive the cleansing He has provided.

The lampstands burned brightly, speaking of the Word of God which is a "light to our feet and a lamp to our path", and our need to have our way constantly lit by it.

The tables of shewbread - the bread of the presence - told of the sweet communion with God which is available to the priests (in the New Covenant, that's all of us who know Jesus as Lord and Saviour!)

Then there was the golden altar, from which incense ascended to God, speaking of the prayer of the saints.

The priests had consecrated themselves, setting themselves apart "for God's use only".

Yes, it was all ready, just waiting for one thing... the presence of God. Then Solomon called for the Ark of the Covenant. The priests carried it in on their shoulders using wooden staves passed through the rings on the side of the Ark. It was set up in the Holy of Holies, beneath the outspread wings of the cherubim (which were, incidentally, not cute little babies with fluffy little wings but huge, magnificent creatures with 15-foot wingspans.)

The musicians worshipped with all they had, coming together in unity before the Lord.

Then the presence of God came, the temple was filled with a cloud, and the priests could not perform their service because of the presence of the Lord.

Yet something was missing from the Ark. 2 Chronicles 6:11 says that the only thing in the Ark was the Law, the two stone tablets which Moses had received on Horeb. However, in the past there had been two other objects in the Ark: the golden pot of manna (Exodus 16:32-33) and Aaron's staff that budded (Numbers 17:10.)

The Law speaks of the character of God. It is fashionable for us to New Testament saints to scoff at the law, to see most of it as irrelevant or even arbitrary. Yet it is neither. The law is not merely a set of rules God made up, as one might make up the rules of a game. Nor did He sit in heaven, scratch His head and say, "Now what can I come up with to make life as difficult as possible for these guys?" No, the law is the expression of His character. The moral law is the expression of His righteousness. The judicial law is an expression of both His justice and His love. The laws regarding separation (food, health etc) are an expression of His holiness, his separateness. The laws about dealing with Gentiles are an expression of His goodness and mercy. The ritual laws concerning the Temple, priesthood and sacrifices are an expression of His redemptive purposes. The commands concerning the judgement of sin, whether in individuals or nations, are an expression of His judgement.

The pot of manna spoke of God's provision for man. In this case, it was specifically material provision, but we can take it as provision in every area of need, whether it be material goods, healing, comfort, joy, peace, anointing, revelation - whatever the need may be, we can see its provision symbolised in the pot of manna. God provided the manner when there were no natural resources available: it was his miraculous provision. His people didn't have to work for it, other than to go out and collect it, and they were guaranteed that no matter how much or how little they collected they would have just enough. If they got greedy or lazy, however, and tried to keep it for the next day, then it would get maggots and stink - except for the Sabbath, when no manna fell, and what they had collected the previous day stayed fresh and palatable.

Aaron's rod that budded was the symbol of God's authority given to his servants. Some of the people of Israel had risen up in rebellion because only Aaron's family, as priests, had the right to come before the Lord to offer sacrifices. They demanded that they should all have this right. God judged them severely (read the story in Numbers 16), then He told the leaders of each of the twelve tribes to bring an almond rod and set it before the Lord. The rod of the man the Lord had chosen would bud, thus vindicating Moses' choice of Aaron. In fact, Aaron's rod not only budded, but blossomed and produced almonds.

However, the jar of manna and Aaron's rod were missing by the time the Ark was brought into the Temple. Who took them? It almost certainly happened during the time that the Ark was in captivity in the land of the Philistines. The Bible doesn't tell us, but we can be certain of one thing: whoever removed them paid with his life. If well-meaning Uzzah was struck down when he tried to steady the Ark which was being moved wrongly (2 Samuel 6:3-7), certainly those who pried open the sacred box to steal from it for their own gratification would have met a most unseemly end.

We can be certain, also, that immediately they were removed from the presence of God the pot of manna would have developed worms and begun to stink terribly, and the rod would have dropped its buds, its blossoms and its almonds and become nothing more than a shrivelled, dry old stick. It was only the presence of God that kept them alive.

So here we have the Ark entering the Temple, minus the pot of manna and minus Aaron's rod that budded. Yet the presence and the glory of God still fell. Why? Because His character were still there, and God's presence is tied up with His character. It is not dependent on His provision for us - God would still be God if He had never given us a single thing. Nor is it dependant on His delegation of authority to us - He would still be God even if He had never given us a single crumb of His authority. Where His character is, His presence is.

Have we, I wonder, been like the Philistines? Have we raided the Ark while it was lost? When there was little sense of the presence of God in the Church, have we snatched the pot of manna, thinking that if we had His provision we had Him? Have we then wondered why the manna got maggots and began to stink? Have we failed to see that the ever-fresh provision of the Lord is to be found only in the presence of the Lord, and His presence is to be found only in His character?

Have we taken God's authority out of His presence, thinking that we can have it without really having Him? Have we then wondered why our authority withered and shrivelled and became nothing more than a dry stick in our hands? Could we not see that God's authority is like a stream of life from the throne, which can come only from His presence and His character?

Worse, have we wrenched the tablets of the law from the Ark, thrown them away and left only the pot of manna and Aaron's rod? Can we really imagine that God's presence would sit on such a throne? Of course not! His presence went with His character, which we threw away.

God is bringing His church into a time when He will manifest His presence in ways which exceed our wildest imaginings. But He will do so only when His character is enthroned in the Ark. He will do so regardless of whether His provision for us, and His authority given to us, is there or not. If we want His provision to be fresh, if we want His authority to be alive, it is up to us to see that they are returned to the Ark, joined to His character and received from His presence.

WISE MEN STILL SEEK HIM

Almost everyone knows the Christmas story of the wise men, although it didn't happen quite as portrayed on the Christmas cards. For a start, it is most unlikely that they visited the baby Jesus in the stable: in fact, it is probable that the only night He actually spent in the stable was the night of His birth. After that, it seems that the little family moved into a house, and it was there that the Magi found them. (Matt 2:11)

What's more, they probably took a couple of years to get there. The Greek word used for "child" means a toddler rather than a baby. This also explains why Herod extended his extermination decree to all children under two years old.

We also don't know for sure that there were three wise men. We know that they brought three different gifts - gold, frankincense and myrrh - but we are not told how many wise men brought the gifts. All we know is that it was more than one.

I mention these things just to get them out of the way, because some people become very hung up on such details. It is good to have the story straight, but when we concentrate on these minor things, it is easy to lose sight of the things that are really important.

What is the important issue of the magi's story? I believe it is that God always paints a much bigger picture than what we see.

Mary and Joseph were ordinary, poor people. (We know they were poor, because when they came to bring the offering at Jesus' dedication they brought two doves, an offering that was allowed only for those who were too poor to bring a lamb.) They lived in obscurity in an ordinary village among other ordinary people. When the census was called they went, with hundreds of other ordinary people, to the small, ordinary town of Bethlehem.

Something amazingly extraordinary had happened to them, and the event itself had been celebrated by angels and couched in miracles. But once the wonder of that night passed, once the angels had returned to the heavenly realms and the shepherds had gone back to tending their flocks, once the little family had moved back to the ordinariness of living in a house like every other family, there must have been times when they wondered how, in the midst of such obscurity, God would ever make these wonders known to the world.

Yet, far away, some wise men saw a star. They knew from the ancient wisdom that God had caused to be written that this star was not like the millions of others they saw every night in the vast blackness of the sky. This star was the portent of the birth of a King who would be unlike any other.

And, armed only with that knowledge and a deep inner compulsion to seek Him, they followed it. For two years through the desert they followed, undeterred by either the harshness of the terrain or the length of the journey.

Mary and Joseph knew nothing of their quest until they arrived at the house. When the magi knocked on the door, what amazement must have filled Mary and Joseph's hearts. What God had seemed to have hidden in obscurity, He had actually made known thousands of miles away.

It may be that you, like Mary and Joseph, feel that you are lost in obscurity. God has done amazing things in your life, but it seems that no-one will ever know about them. Your destiny seems limited by the smallness of your surroundings.

But God has painted a picture far bigger than you can see or imagine. Just as He caused the revelation about the star to be written hundreds of years before the event; just as He caused the right people - the magi - to discover that revelation at exactly the right time; and just as He placed in their hearts the burning desire to seek Him; so He has gone ahead of you and is able to bring together all the people and events necessary to cause your light to be seen.

No matter where they are, and no matter how hard or long the journey, those whose hearts are for God will always pursue Him. Wise men will always seek Him, and if He is working in your life they will find Him in you.

YOU'RE NOT HOME YET!

There is a story about a missionary couple in the early part of the twentieth century. Having reached retirement age, and been replaced on the field by a younger couple, they were returning by ship to the USA. On the same voyage was a famous movie star, returning after an "on location" shoot in Africa.

When the ship berthed at their destination, the movie star and her entourage were first on the gangplank. Hordes of press and radio representatives were there to greet her, along with a huge crowd of excited fans. The dock was decorated in welcome, a band played, and cameras flashed everywhere. After the star had entered a limousine and been driven away, the media representatives scurried off to lodge their stories and the crowd of fans dispersed.

Sometime later the missionary couple came to walk down the gangplank. No one was there to greet them or to carry their luggage, no one was interested to hear their story. In their hearts they cried out to God, "Lord, there has been all this fuss and to-do to welcome home this movie star. But for us, who have labored faithfully for You all these years, there is nothing." Then they heard the gentle, loving voice of the Father: "My son, My daughter, you're not home yet!"

This story has often spoken to my heart. At one time Christianity was totally heaven-focused. We sang about "When the roll is called up yonder" and "In the sweet bye and bye". We looked for our rewards not here in this present life, but in the life of eternity.

Then someone decided, "We don't want 'pie in the sky bye and bye when you die', we want 'steak on your plate while you wait'." The emphasis changed. No longer were God's people content to wait for eternity for their rewards. Like little children, we wanted it now! Suddenly, being a Christian had to mean success, prosperity and material fulfillment in this life.

Now certainly there is a truth that God desires to bless us. Sometimes, though, I wonder whether maybe God uses a different dictionary to the one we use. His definition of blessing sometimes seems very different from ours. I also wonder whether, in pursuing our definition of blessing, we may be missing out on the greater good which is His definition of blessing.

Paul wrote, "If we have only hoped in Christ in this life, we are of all men most pitiable." (1 Cor. 15:19) Is this really true of us? In looking at the Christianity of the early 21st century, especially the variety taught and practised in the western nations, it seems to me that for many of us, it is not. Many of us could say that, even if we have been wrong and death is the end of everything, our lives have been such that no one would look at them and say that we have missed out on anything.

Yet there are large parts of the Church today whose experience is vastly different. Their faith is costly. For them, belief in Christ can mean everything from loss of employment to loss of life. It can mean imprisonment, torture, and insult. It can mean being disowned and declared dead by their families. To them, a "prosperity gospel" is meaningless. Faith, for them, is not a button to be pushed in order to make a vending-machine god produce whatever they want. Rather, faith is measured in terms of faithfulness, and is hammered out on the anvil of suffering.

I believe they are vastly richer in God than those of us who live with the sanitised, God-will-give-you-whatever-you-want Christianity of the west. I envy them the grittiness and moment-to-moment dependence on God of their walk. I envy them the vitality and reality of their faith. I envy them the clarity of their understanding that our hope in Christ is not just for this life, but for eternity.

No, I am not seeking to promote a morbid and depressing Christianity. There is much in this life that is joyous and beautiful: birdsong and music, nature and art, friends' company and grandchildren's hugs. More than that, our faith itself should be a source of tremendous joy in this life. In the midst of it, however, let us remember that this life is not our destiny, but only the journey to our destiny.

Some years ago I wrote a song expressing my understanding of this. The chorus says,

I've got heaven on my mind, I'm coming home;
I've got heaven on my mind, I'm coming home;
This old earth has much to give
And I delight to live
But I've got heaven on my mind
I'm coming home.

We're not home yet!

THE FEAR OF THE LORD

The Word of God tells us that "the fear of the Lord is the beginning of wisdom." Many in the Church today want to water that down to "reverential awe", insisting that fear and faith are incompatible, and that "perfect love casts out fear."

I have many times experienced "reverential awe." It is, in my understanding, a natural component of worship. When I begin to focus on God – His greatness, His power, His glory, His majesty, His beauty, His awesomeness – I simply can't help but be overawed by Him.

Often I am reminded of the apostle John. During Jesus' earthly life, John was "the beloved disciple", the one who was closest to Him. It was John that sat next to Jesus at the last supper, reclining against Him in a gesture of intimate friendship. Yet when that same John saw the glorified Christ in his Patmos vision, his immediate reaction was to fall on his face in worship.

I have joked many times that, being the person I am, when I finally get to heaven I will probably burst through the gates like an excited schoolgirl yelling "Hey Daddy! I'm home!" That may be true, but everything in me knows that, as intimate and tender as my relationship with the Lord has been here on earth, when I see Him as He is I, like John, will be flat on my face.

That reverential awe is a vital part of our Christian experience. It lifts us above the circumstances that surround us, and reminds us that we serve a God who is bigger than anything that the world, the flesh or the devil can throw at us. It reminds us that God is not our servant, a push-button vending machine that will give us anything we ask for; nor is He some kind of doting grandfather who will ignore our sin and simply pat us on the head and smile when we do wrong. He is the King of the universe, and it is good for us to encounter Him as such on a regular basis.

However, as important and as wonderful as that reverential awe is, it is not "the fear of the Lord." As I said, I have experienced reverential awe many times, and I expect to experience it many times more before I go home. I have experienced the fear of the Lord only once, and I will never forget it for all eternity.

Let me emphasise that I am not "afraid" of God. I have an absolutely open and honest relationship with Him. If I am upset about something, I tell Him – often in far-from-gracious terms. Yes, I generally end up having to repent later, but I don't see the point of pretending to be ok with something if I'm not. After all, He already knows what is going on in my heart anyway. If I were to slip into religious mode and tell Him that I accept His will when I am really not yet prepared to, I'm sure He would clip me across the back of the head and tell me to stop lying to Him. God is big enough to handle my grumbles – and even the occasional flat-out temper tantrum – and He knows that my heart for Him means that I will always yield to Him after I have done the dummy-spit.

Once, though, I pushed the envelope just a tiny fraction too far. I can't remember what it was about, or even what I said to Him, but I know I stepped over the line. As I did, I heard the Lord utter an almost audible "Oh, is that right?" Then, for the briefest moment, He pulled back the corner of the mantle of His grace that covers me, and I caught the tiniest glimpse of what it feels like to stand stark naked before the righteousness and judgement of the holy – and angry – God. What I experienced in that fleeting instant was not reverential awe. It was sheer, stark, unadulterated, mind-numbing terror.

Did the experience change my relationship with God to one of fear rather than faith? No, if anything it made my faith stronger as I marvel at the protection and covering provided for me by the blood of Jesus. Did I lose the intimacy that I had with Father? No, if anything I am closer to Him, knowing that His love means that I don't have to experience that terror – in infinitely greater measure – for all eternity. I delight in the closeness and tenderness of my relationship with Him more than ever, but I know with greater certainty than I ever did that my relationship with Him exists only within the covering of His grace. It is by His grace alone that I am able to stand in His presence, and I love Him all the more for extending that grace to me. I certainly never want to venture outside of that covering! Do I still yell at God from time to time? Most definitely – but I now understand that there is a line past which intimacy becomes impudence and a tantrum becomes treason, and it is my most sincere prayer that I will never cross it again.

I pray that every Christian would experience the reverential awe of God many times in their lives; but also that every Christian would, at least once, truly experience the fear of the Lord. If they did, the depth of relationship with God throughout the Body of Christ would be greatly increased.

MEET THE AUTHOR

I don't remember a time when I didn't write. My Dad was an Australian bush poet, and words on paper were always part of my life. At the same time, I never held an ambition to be a writer - it was just something I did.

I was dramatically saved in 1974, and called straight into ministry. From that point forward my writing became part of my ministry. During the 70s, 80s and 90s I had quite a few articles published in print magazines, and with the coming of the internet most of my writing moved online.

This collection is my eighth published book, but at the time of releasing this most of them are out of print because I closed my publishing business. I am in the process of re-releasing most of them through KOGMI Books.

I currently head up King of Glory Ministries International, an apostolic ministry based in Australia, where I live. Through KOGMI I am "Mum Lynn" to a growing network of pastors and churches around the world.

I'm also natural Mum and Grandma to two sons, five grandchildren and three foster grandchildren.

www.ingramcontent.com/pod-product-compliance
Lightning Source LLC
Chambersburg PA
CBHW072007070526
44583CB00015B/1370